King Cole

KING COLE

A picture portrait of Sir Henry Cole, KCB 1808–1882

Elizabeth Bonython

The publication of this book has been made possible by
generous contributions from the Associates of the V & A
and the Royal Society of Arts

Victoria and Albert Museum

© Copyright of text Elizabeth Bonython
© Illustrations as listed
ISBN 0–905209–19–2

Edited by Anthony Burton
Designed by HMSO Graphic Design

Printed in England for HMSO
by Balding & Mansell Ltd. Wisbech
Typesetting by Unwin Bros. Ltd.
The Gresham Press, Woking and London
D/d No. 8219780

Foreword

It is particularly appropriate that the first book to be written about the founder of this museum should appear in the year that marks the centenary of his death. It is equally appropriate that it is being published by the V & A, his own creation, jointly with the Royal Society of Arts and with the assistance of the Associates of the V & A. The V & A and RSA, with which he was so closely associated, thus acknowledge their debt to Cole by publishing this short book which will make him familiar to a public that unknowingly owes him so much. Had he not been inspired by a tireless zeal to help his fellow men the Penny Post would not have been introduced when it was, nor would the Royal Albert Hall have been built. Without South Kensington with its museums, science and art colleges and music schools, London would be a poorer place today. It is strange that this brilliant man, who made such radical reforms in so many fields, has never been accorded his proper place as one of the greatest innovators of the Victorian age, and has been almost totally neglected by historians. This book will hopefully represent a first step in his restoration to the pantheon of the nineteenth century.

Roy Strong
Director

Acknowledgements

I should like to begin by thanking Sir Henry Cole's descendants for the help I have had from them. His great grand-daughter, Cynthia Dutnall (Mrs Roger Dutnall) has, by her generosity and friendship, made the work for this book a pleasure. Léah Grillard, (Madame Marcel Grillard), who is descended from both Cole and Francis Fowke had me to stay at her seaside house in Normandy, while I tried to read Frank Fowke's tiny writing that he used in his diary. Other members of the family who have lent me precious photographs and papers are Mrs Bartley, Dr Susan Cole, Mrs Herbert, Mr Fowke Mangeot and Mrs Josephine Seccombe.

Among my friends at the Victoria and Albert Museum I am especially grateful to Anthony Burton, Shirley Bury and John Physick, who have been my mentors for many years. Much of this book is the fruit of their scholarly research, and it would have been a poor thing without their help. Others at the museum whom I would like to thank are—Harold Barkley, Isabel Beattie, Claude Blair, Anne Buddle, Martin Chapman, Avril Hart, Mark Haworth Booth, Christina Huntley, Lionel Lambourne, Julian Litten, John Murdoch, Frances Newton, Michael Snodin, Moira Thunder, Eric Turner, Irene Weller and Irene Whalley. Nicky Bird, the Publications Officer, has always been encouraging, when it seemed that this book would never be published. The photographs were taken by Graham Brandon, Sally Chappell and Christine Smith.

I have had a good deal of help from the staff of other institutions, and I am particularly grateful to Sarah Wimbush at the National Portrait Gallery; Shona Angus at the Scottish National Portrait Gallery; and Miss Clare Lambert, Secretary of the Gilbert and Sullivan Society.

A number of people have most kindly answered my questions, or allowed me to read their family papers: They are—Lady Bragg and her daughter Patience Thompson, for Sir Philip Cunliffe-Owen; Mrs Molesworth-St Aubyn, for Sir William Molesworth; Mrs Barker, for Sir Francis Palgrave; Mr Gerald Robinson, Mrs Goble, Mrs Hockliffe and Mr Quentin Hockliffe, for Sir Charles Robinson. Also Caroline Haworth and Alan Hills. Material from the Royal Archives, which is subject to copyright, is republished by gracious permission of Her Majesty the Queen.

Contents

The Essay   1

The Illustrations   13

Index   67

Illustrations

Front cover
  'King Cole'
  Coloured engraving after James Tissot
  Vanity Fair, 1871

Back cover
  Henry Cole
  Pen drawing by Richard Doyle, c.1865
  British Museum

Frontispiece
  Henry Cole
  Portrait photograph by Melluish, c.1870
  Victoria and Albert Museum

1   The Writing School at Christ's Hospital
    Aquatint by J C Stadler, 1816
    Victoria and Albert Museum

2   Sir Francis Palgrave
    Pencil drawing by Elizabeth Turner,
      1819
    Victoria and Albert Museum

3   'See the Conquering hero (heroine)
      Comes'
    Anonymous pen drawing
    Cole family

4   Thomas Love Peacock
    Photograph by Mayall, 1857
    The Works of Thomas Love Peacock,
      edited by Henry Cole, 1875

5   John Stuart Mill
    Photograph, c.1865
    National Portrait Gallery

6   Sir William Molesworth
    Lithograph by Daniel Maclise, 1838
    Fraser's Magazine

7   Charles Buller
    Engraving
    Part 1 of John Saunders' *Political
      Reformers* 1837

8   Lord Langdale
    Miniature by H Collen, 1829
    National Portrait Gallery

9   Henry and Marian Cole in 1855
    Photograph
    Cole family

10 Henry and Marian Cole with their
      children
    Photograph, c.1858
    Cole family

11 Rowland Hill
    Posthumous portrait by J A Vintner
    National Portrait Gallery

12 'The Edinburgh Mail'
    Wood engraving after Henry Cole, 1839
    The Post Circular

13 The postage cover
    Engraving after William Mulready, 1840
    Victoria and Albert Museum

14 William Mulready
    Portrait by John Linnell, 1833
    National Portrait Gallery

15 Maria Callcott
    Sketch by Sir Thomas Lawrence, 1819
    National Portrait Gallery

16 The first Christmas Card
    Engraving after J C Horsley
    Fifty Years of Public Work, by Henry
      Cole, 1884

17 Richard Redgrave
    Self-portrait, c.1830
    National Portrait Gallery

18a John Bell
    Engraving from *The Illustrated London
      News*, 1895

18b The Felix Summerly bread board

19 '"Come, let's to bed", says Sleepy-head',
    Lithograph by John Linnell, 1843
    Traditional Nursery Songs of England,
       by Felix Summerly, 1843

20 W M Thackeray
    Pencil drawing by Daniel Maclise, c.1832
    Garrick Club

21 C Wentworth Dilke
    Engraving from *The Illustrated London
       News*, 1851

22 John Scott Russell
    Portrait by H W Phillips, c.1855
    Scottish National Portrait Gallery

23 Herbert Minton
    Portrait. Painter unknown, c.1855
    Minton Museum and Royal Doulton Ltd.

24 The Felix Summerly Tea-set
    Victoria and Albert Museum

25 Collection of Felix Summerly
       Art-Manufactures
    Victoria and Albert Museum

26 Albert, Prince Consort of England
    Coloured lithograph, after Winterhalter,
       1855
    Private Collection

27 Lord Granville
    Photograph, c.1856
    Cole family

28 Lyon Playfair
    Engraving by T Maguire, 1851
    National Portrait Gallery

29 The Organisers of the Great Exhibition
    Group portrait by H W Phillips, 1853
    Victoria and Albert Museum

30 The Opening of the Great Exhibition
    Painting by H C Selous, 1852
    Victoria and Albert Museum

31 Valentine, 1852
    Pen and wash drawing by W M
       Thackeray, 1852
    Cole family

32 Marlborough House, a gallery in the
       Museum of Ornamental Art
    Water-colour by W L Casey, 1857
    Victoria and Albert Museum

33 The Funeral of the Duke of Wellington
    Coloured Lithograph by T Picken, 1852
    Victoria and Albert Museum

34 Sir (John) Charles Robinson
    Miniature by W Maw Egley, 1852
    Robinson family

35 Sir (Francis) Philip Cunliffe-Owen
    Photograph
    From *Men of Mark*, 1880

36 Captain Francis Fowke R E
    Photograph, c.1860
    Cole family

37 Major-General H Y D Scott R E
    Engraving from *The Illustrated London
       News*, 1883

38 Elm Cottage, Shere
    (a) In 1856
    (b) In about 1860
         Photographs by Henry Cole
    Cole family

39 (Francis) Seymour Haden
    Etching, self-portrait, 1862
    National Portrait Gallery

40 The Grounds of the South Kensington
       Museum in 1862
    Water colour by Anthony Stannus, 1862
    Victoria and Albert Museum

41 Robert Lowe
    Portrait by G F Watts, c.1870
    National Portrait Gallery

42 The Memorial to the Great Exhibition
    Water colour by Anthony Stannus, 1861
    Victoria and Albert Museum

43 The Opening of the Royal Horticultural
       Society's Gardens
    Water colour by E Walker, 1861
    Victoria and Albert Museum

44 The Royal Horticultural Society's
       Gardens from the North
    Water colour by E Walker, 1863
    Victoria and Albert Museum

45 The Prince of Wales
    Carte de visite photograph, 1868
    National Portrait Gallery

46 General, the Honble Charles Grey
    Portrait by Sir Francis Grant, 1869
    Private Collection

47 The Royal Albert Hall
    Photograph, 1868
    Cole family

48 The Loggia of the Science Schools
    Photograph, c.1872
    Victoria and Albert Museum

49 Sir Joseph Whitworth, Bart.
    Engraving from *The Yearbook of Facts
    in Science and Art*, 1869

50 The 3rd Duke of Sutherland
    Carte de visite photograph, c.1861
    National Portrait Gallery

51 Sewage at Rochdale
    Water colour by Frank Fowke, 1877
    Victoria and Albert Museum

52 The Honble (Edward) Frederick
    Leveson-Gower
    Engraving from *Harriet, Countess
    Granville*, by Susan Oldfield, 1901

53 Group of Staff members at the South
    Kensington Museum
    Photograph, c.1860
    Victoria and Albert Museum

54 The entrance to the museum in 1872
    Water colour by C E Emery, 1872
    Victoria and Albert Museum

55 'King Cole'
    Coloured engraving after James Tissot
    Vanity Fair, 1871

Illustrations in the essay

1   Cole aged 12 in 1820
    Silhouette, artist unknown
    Cole family

2   Cole aged about 27, c.1835
    Drawing, artist unknown
    Cole family

3   Cole aged 37 in 1846
    Portrait miniature by John Simpson
    Cole family

4   Cole at the time of the Great Exhibition
    Engraving from *The Illustrated London
    News*, 1851

5   Marlborough House
    Engraving, c.1855

6   Charles Dickens
    Portrait by W P Frith, 1859 (detail)
    Victoria and Albert Museum

7   Cole aged 57 in 1865
    Drawing by Samuel Laurence (detail)
    National Portrait Gallery

T wo national institutions remain today as memorials to the work and personality of Sir Henry Cole: they are the Royal Albert Hall and the Victoria and Albert Museum. Even the part of London where they both stand was given its name and its identity by him. The Albert Hall owes its existence, and its continually shaky finances, almost wholly to Cole. It was his idea to have a concert hall, as well as the memorial in Kensington Gardens, to commemorate Queen Victoria's consort, who died in 1861. It was also his idea to pay for the construction of the hall by selling 'sittings' and boxes outright to freeholders. This resulted in so little money being taken at the box office that the managers have had difficulties ever since.

1   Cole aged 12 in 1820

Down the road from the Albert Hall is the Victoria and Albert Museum, one of the great art museums of the world. Cole was its first director, and he built it up from a small collection of objects bought by the government from the Great Exhibition of 1851. The first building for the museum was put up in the mid-fifties, next door to the parish church of Brompton. When Cole moved in he got the Prince Consort's approval to call it the South Kensington Museum. He knew that in people's minds Brompton was a depressing place, low-lying and damp. Kensington had an altogether more light and pleasant feel; on high ground; on gravel rather than London clay; and, with its palace and gardens, a more fashionable part of London. The Queen changed the museum's name to the Victoria and Albert in 1899, but South Kensington has continued as the name for the area, and the old village of Brompton is forgotten.

Cole's contemporaries might have said that his greatest achievement was the part he played in conceiving and organising the 1851 Exhibition: the first-ever international exhibition. It was he who first suggested to Prince Albert that it should be an international, rather than a domestic one. He was given the unenviable task of dividing the space inside the Crystal Palace among the 14,000 exhibitors. He managed it by hard work, cajolery, and by simply over-riding anyone who complained.

He got things done, but he was not liked. Lord Derby, who was Prime Minister when Cole was collecting names of subscribers to the

Albert Hall, called him 'the most generally unpopular man I know'. Many people assumed that he had made a fortune out of the Exhibition and from land-speculation after it. From the 1830s down to the 1980s, Cole has received a bad press, if he has been noticed at all. At least one well-known painter, J C Horsley, whom Cole helped when he was a young man, and who designed Cole's Christmas card, omits him altogether from his two volumes of recollections. Even in 1909, when Cole's grand design for the museum was completed by Sir Aston Webb, and the new buildings facing Cromwell Road were opened by King Edward VII, there was no mention of Cole in the speeches. *The Times* paid tribute to his old adversary, Sir Charles Robinson, who was still alive, which drew a letter of complaint from Cole's admirer, Sir Henry Trueman Wood, the secretary of the Royal Society of Arts.

In fact, Cole was of a small band of nineteenth-century Victorian reformers, who dedicated themselves wholly to the public good. He was a Utilitarian, and as a young man had been close to John Stuart Mill, John Roebuck, Charles Buller, William Molesworth, and Edwin Chadwick. Chadwick lived in Cole's house with him for about a year in the late 1830s. Cole was hopelessly altruistic and high-minded and failed to take opportunities to make money to the extent of leaving his widow and unmarried daughters hardly provided for. At his death, his estate amounted to £7,000 and the government had to give Lady Cole a pension of £250 a year.

Cole's fundamentally warm personality was masked, in public life, by a hectoring manner, so that over and over again his close friends and colleagues had to warn him to be less overbearing and more gentle with people. It says much for his nature that his friends felt able to offer such advice. Towards the end of his life, when perhaps he had softened a little, he was often mistaken for Lord Houghton (Richard Monkton-Milnes) who was well-known for his affability.

Cole was a smiling man, short, athletic and bespectacled. It is a great pity that portraits and photographs usually show him looking serious. His spectacles are always omitted, which could be owing to his own vanity. He was one of those people who always look crumpled however carefully they dress themselves; he invariably had a coloured handkerchief dangling untidily from his coat-tail pocket. By the time he was forty-five his hair had gone white, and he wore it and his whiskers unfashionably long, so that the effect was of a quick-striding man, clothes and mane flying. A little dog was his constant companion, yapping and scampering along the museum galleries, its toes clicking on the mosaic floors.

Henry Cole—he had no middle name—was the son of a young Dragoon officer who had been badly wounded during the riots in Dublin in 1801. Unfit for active service, Henry Robert Cole toured the Country as a recruiting officer. Cole had early memories of riding on the pommel of his father's saddle, dressed as a miniature dragoon in red tunic and gold braid. Cole said of himself that he was 'a thoroughly spoilt child'. When he was about two, he cried all night for the moon and both his parents promised it to him. 'But the moon went down and I was not pacified. I have wanted other moons in later life without getting them: but this was the first time and shows influences which started me on my career. . . . My Will has always seemed to be my most marked possession. . . . for years I have fixed on some decision until said Will had its own way'. Cole said, when comparing his own upbringing with that of John Stuart Mill, that his parents 'encouraged the cultivation of the feelings'.

At the end of the Napoleonic Wars, recruiting ceased and the Cole family came to London to live by the river at Chelsea. Henry was sent to Christ's Hospital [1]*. There he won a silver medal for writing, with the result that in 1823 he got employment as a clerk to Sir Francis Palgrave [2], a sub-commissioner of the Record Commission. For nine years he worked for Sir Francis, transcribing ancient documents and preparing them for publication. From 1832 to 1835 he worked directly under the secretary of the Record Commission. This man, a barrister, who boasted over and over again that he knew nothing about the public records, at first encouraged Cole to call himself a sub-commissioner and put him in charge of the Augmentation Office (a department established by Henry VIII when his revenue was augmented as a result of the dissolution of the monasteries). Then he changed his mind, told Cole that he was only a clerk and could not claim the increased salary that had been promised. Their quarrel ended in Cole being dismissed.

Since about 1828, when there had been an undignified wrangle at the Society of Antiquaries, the enormities of the Record Commission were gradually being made public. It became known that the Commission was inefficient and wasted large sums of money, while the commissioners made no attempt to make any improvements. Once Cole was no longer a civil servant, he was free to bring his opposition to the whole system out into the open. He turned to his friends, T L Peacock [4], John Mill [5], William Molesworth [6] and Charles Buller [7]. Together they orchestrated a campaign of pamphlets and letters to the papers – Cole became adept at answering his own letters, using several false names – which ended in a Select Committee of the House of Commons being granted in 1836.

Two years later, when the fuss had died down, Lord Langdale [8] re-instated Cole as an Assistant-Keeper in charge of the Augmentation Office, and of the records stored at Carlton Ride. Officially, Cole remained employed by the Record Commission until the beginning of 1852, when he transferred to the Board of Trade. The affair of the

2 Cole aged about 27, c. 1835

---

* The outline of Henry Cole's career is given in this essay. The figures in brackets refer to the illustrations between pages 14 and 65. They are mostly about the people he knew and the captions give details about them. A few illustrations are not mentioned at all in the text.

public records made Cole famous, some might have said infamous. He learnt the uses of journalism and publicity, and people in high places began to hear of him. It was known that Cole was close to the Philosophic Radicals and a particular friend of John Mill. To the Whigs he was becoming known as a useful man, a man of ideas, who was prepared to work hard and carry his ideas to results. To the high Tories he was a dangerous trouble-maker. This did not worry Cole, who never let such things prey on him: back at the public records, he married his first cousin, Marian Bond [9], and had a baby girl.

In the same year, 1838, Cole met Rowland Hill [11], and helped him to introduce his scheme for a cheap pre-paid letter post. It was because Cole was put in charge of getting the postage cover designed [13], that he met William Mulready [14] and then other painters: Richard Redgrave [17], Thomas Webster, Daniel Maclise, H J Townsend, J C Horsley and the sculptor, John Bell [18]. Many of these new friends taught at the Government School of Design in London and were involved in its rows and failures. Later on, the reform of the design schools all over the country was to be one of Cole's greatest successes.

By 1843, Cole and his wife had two daughters who were beginning to need picture books. He found none that pleased him, so he wrote a series of nearly twenty, which was published as *The Home Treasury*. They were intended to 'cultivate the Affections, Fancy, Imagination, and Taste of Children', and he persuaded his painter friends to illustrate them [19]. He adopted the *nom de plume* of Felix Summerly for this and other commercial ventures. He used the name, too, as a *nom de guerre* for some of his pamphlets and letters to the papers. Between 1843 and 1851, Cole as Summerly wrote children's books, guide books to historic buildings such as Westminster Abbey and Hampton Court, and catalogues to picture galleries. In 1846 he began to ask his artist friends to design pretty objects of everyday use, together with some parian china figures, which he launched commercially under the style of 'Felix Summerly's Art-Manufacturers'.

The late 1830s and the 1840s were the age of the train. Investing money in the railways amounted to a mania. Companies sprang up to cover the country with a disorganised network of lines. Cole realised that as the companies were independent of each other, and used tracks of different widths, the system would never run efficiently. He foresaw, too, that traffic was bound to increase and that separate lines would be needed to carry passengers and goods. He joined in the campaign to make the changes that were needed, writing pamphlets, and letters and articles in magazines. He persuaded his friend W M Thackeray [20] to write a 'Jeames Yellowplush' adventure for *Punch*, ridiculing the inconveniences of having to change trains at Gloucester.

One of the magazines for which Cole wrote at this time was *The Railway Chronicle*, a weekly paper, run by Wentworth Dilke [21] and

John Scott Russell [22]. Russell was Secretary of the Society for the Encouragement of Arts Manufacturers and Commerce. Cole joined the Society early in 1846, caused many of his friends to join and began to make changes. Soon he and his supporters had 'packed' the Council, and Cole was elected chairman in 1850 and again in 1852. For many years, he had almost complete control over the Society. He instituted the weekly journal and used it and the weight of the Society's prestige to further whatever reform he happened to have uppermost in his mind. He called it 'a society that pokes its nose into everything', and right up to within a few weeks of his death he was busy on its Council and committees. The subjects he chiefly pursued– apart from the Great Exhibitions of 1851 and 1862, which hold pride of place–were patents and the rights of inventors, the founding of a territorial army, the extension of postal reform to include overseas and parcel post, the development of the Society's examinations in technical subjects, the improvement of health in towns by better drainage and water supply, musical education, domestic economy and cookery, to name only a few. Sir Henry Trueman Wood, in his history of the Society, wrote: 'He [Cole] was not a skilful or a cautious financier. Certain of his schemes cost the Society dear, but if he wasted some of its funds, it was mainly due to him that the Society had funds to waste.'

Prince Albert [26] was elected President of the Society in 1843, and (to quote Wood again) 'he continuously impressed on the Society the necessity of its taking steps to improve the condition of the artistic industries of the country, then in a very backward condition, and . . . urged on the Society, as its proper work, the encouragement of the application of art to practical purposes'.

Already, the French often held trade fairs, and triennial exhibitions were held in Dublin. So 'steps were taken by those who directed the Society's action to prepare the public mind for a great national exhi- bition'. As a beginning, three small one-day exhibitions were held in the winter of 1844–5, but little notice was taken of them. It needed the flair and energy of Cole and Russell to make the exhibitions a success and to educate the 'public mind' to support the idea of a large exhibition of British goods.

The first exhibition which Cole and Russell organised was held in the Spring of 1846, where Herbert Minton [23] won a medal, and Cole, as Felix Summerly Esq., won a prize for a tea service [24]. It was this success which encouraged him to begin his little business of Felix Summerly's Art-Manufacturer, and he went on to exhibit at the Society's exhibitions of 1847, 1848, and 1849. Each one was more popular than the last, and the one held in 1849 was visited by nearly 100,000 people.

That summer the Society sent Matthew Digby Wyatt, the archi- tect, to Paris to see the French National Exhibition, and report on whether a similar one could be held in London. Cole went with him,

3   Cole aged 37 in 1846

and in Paris they met Herbert Minton [23] and discussed whether the proposed exhibition in London might not be an international one. A few weeks later, at a meeting at Buckingham Palace, Cole suggested to Prince Albert that the exhibition might be international, and he approved of the idea. Cole and several other members of the Society made hectic tours of industrial towns to persuade businessmen to exhibit and to subscribe to the guarantee fund. In October Cole represented the Prince at a meeting at the Mansion House. It was his first public speech, so he asked C W Dilke to signal to him from the back of the hall if he could not be heard.

It was quite clear that the exhibition was going to be far too large for the Society alone to manage, so, in January 1850, the Queen appointed a Royal Commission, with Prince Albert as President and Lord Granville as Chairman [27]. Cole and Wentworth Dilke were on the Executive Committee, with Digby Wyatt as Secretary. John Scott Russell was appointed as secretary of the Commission.

The Commission was made up of many of the same people who had been on the Record Commission. It was a huge committee, and though the members attended meetings, few of them felt the need to go so far as to do anything They were so suspicious of Cole that they refused to have any member of the Executive Committee sit in at their meetings. The President of the Board of Trade arranged for William Reid, a colonel of the Royal Engineers, to be chairman of the Executive Committee, but well-trained soldier that he was, he was content to wait for orders.

For almost six months nothing was done. Commissioners, Sub-commissioners, committees and sub-committees were appointed, but no building was begun, and no money was promised. There was unexpected opposition to having the exhibition in Hyde Park, and people feared that the crowds would be unruly. The Prince very nearly gave up and Cole worked himself up into a fury, and was only prevented from resigning by the tactfulness of Lyon Playfair [28]. In the end, as is well known, Paxton designed his wonderful greenhouse and the Great Exhibition of the Industry of All Nations opened triumphantly on 1 May 1851 [30].

To everyone's surprise, the Exhibition made a profit of £186,000. Guided by the Prince, and with Government help, the Commissioners purchased some houses and market gardens that lay to the South of Hyde Park; about eighty-six acres in all. The Prince wanted to bring the National Gallery, museums, colleges and learned societies together here into what nowadays would be called a 'centre'. As soon as the land was bought, the Commissioners laid out four elegant streets bordering the main rectangle of their estate, which are now known as Exhibition Road, Cromwell Road, Queens Gate and Kensington Gore. The Prince insisted that they be planted with avenues of trees. This 'South Kensington' estate was to be the scene of Cole's future career.

Just before the Great Exhibition closed, the Government spent £5,000 on exhibits to form the nucleus of an inspirational museum for the Schools of Design, which were still enfeebled and hardly functioning after the constant disputes of the 1840s. At about this time Lord Granville [27] offered Cole the secretaryship of the schools. The appointment was confirmed in February 1852, with Cole being given the title of General Superintendent, and Richard Redgrave [17] that of Art Superintendent in a new department of the Board of Trade, the Department of Practical Art. About a year later, science-education was added to art-education, and the department was renamed the Department of Science and Art. Lyon Playfair [28] was secretary for Science and Cole was put in charge of Art. The depart-ment was no longer under the Board of Trade, but was answerable to the Committee of the Privy Council on Education. Cole made sure that his department was responsible directly to the Lord President of the Council, side-stepping the civil servants, through whom it was customary to have access to his Lordship and to the Vice-President.

Within a few days of his appointment, Cole arranged with Prince Albert to borrow rooms at Marlborough House, a royal residence near Buckingham Palace, and installed his office there with the Schools of Design and their little museum, the Museum of Manufactures' [32]. He began to recruit staff to teach in the schools, to go round the country as school inspectors and to administer the department. One of the new teachers was Charles Robinson [34] one of the first people to understand and study Italian Renaissance art. He soon moved to be in charge of the museum, and later built up its magnificent collec-tion of sculpture. Colonel Henry Cunliffe-Owen of the Royal Engi-neers, became an inspector of schools, after working in the detach-ment of twelves officers and two companies of Sappers that ran the practical side of the Great Exhibition. Owen, who was the elder brother of Philip Cunliffe-Owen [35], was the first of a number of Engineer officers seconded to the department from the War Office. Some of them spent most of their working life in the department, and reached high rank. Scott, Festing and Donnelly, who all joined Cole's team after the move to South Kensington, rose to be major-generals. It seems to this writer that Scott may well have been the butt of W S Gilbert's wit in the Major-General's song from *The Pirates of Penzance*. The words of the song imply that the general, like Scott, has never seen active service:

> 'When I have learnt what progress has been made in
>   modern gunnery,
> When I know more of tactics than a novice in a nunnery,
> In short, when I've a smattering of elemental strategy,
> You'll say a better Major-General has never *sat a*
>   *gee*.
> But still in matters vegetable, animal and mineral,
> I am the very model of a modern Major-General.'

4   Cole at the time of
the Great Exhibition

When Gilbert and Sullivan were writing the *Pirates* in the late 1870s, Arthur Sullivan was principal of the National Training School for Music at South Kensington, and it seems possible that the eccentric workings of the department gave them the idea for the song. The other two major-generals are less likely candidates, for neither of them was a general at that time; and both of them had proved themselves to be brave men: Donnelly had been recommended for the Victoria Cross during the Crimean War, and Festing had served in India during the Mutiny. Both were brought into the department work with another Engineer Officer, Captain Francis Fowke, on the new buildings at South Kensington. Later they both turned towards science, and Donnelly became Secretary of the Department in 1884. Festing was appointed the first Director of the Science Museum when it was separated from the South Kensington Museum in 1893. Fowke [36] and Scott [37] were the two who worked most closely with Cole. Fowke acted as the department's architect and built up the design team that was responsible for the museum's buildings and for buildings elsewhere on the Commissioners' estate, and after his death in 1865, Scott took over and continued at the museum until 1882.

In 1852, very soon after his appointment, Cole set up the Circulating Collections, which toured the provincial Schools of Design in horsedrawn waggons. They expanded into the Circulation Department which survived until 1977, when Government economies brought about its closing. At the same time Cole realised the educative possibilities of photography, and sent out photographs of works of art as part of the circulating collections. Once the move was made to South Kensington, a studio was set up, sappers were trained as photographers, and photographs of objects in the museum were sold

5 Marlborough House

8

to the public. C Thurston Thompson was the official photographer. He was the son of Cole's old friend, John Thompson, and he married Marian Cole's sister, Charlotte Bond, in 1857.

That was the year in which the museum opened at South Kensington. By 1855 Marlborough House had become too small, even though wooden huts were put up in the courtyard. Also the house would soon be needed for the Prince of Wales, who would have his own household after his royal coming-of-age in 1859. The Commissioners of the Exhibition of 1851, therefore, put up a large, cheap, corrugated-iron shed on the South-East corner of their estate. Officially called the Iron Museum, it was reviled for its ugliness and nicknamed the Brompton Boilers. Cole was blamed for it, even though it was planned and built while he was away in Paris, working on the International Exhibition of 1855. He called it 'that unlucky iron shed' and later referred to it as a 'refuge for destitute collections'. There were some old houses standing nearby, which were done up as offices and residences for the staff and the wooden huts were re-erected for the Schools of Design.

6   Charles Dickens

To Cole, the museum was the most important part of his work: he called it his 'child'. He believed museums to be 'antidotes to brutality and vice'. To encourage 'the people' to come in and have their taste and morals improved, he arranged for the museum to be open free on certain evenings, sometimes until ten o'clock. The museum was the first in the world to be lit by gas, and in one gallery there were even gas flares outside the windows, so that the modern stained glass could be seen at night. In Cole's day, the museum held collections which now belong to the Science Museum, and there were galleries showing, among other things, food and building materials.

The work of setting up the museum at South Kensington, added to the general work of the department, made Cole so worn out and thin that his doctor, Seymour Haden [39], and the royal physician Sir James Clark, advised him to go to Italy for a year. Characteristically, he was away for only six months. Equally characteristically, he made purchases for the museum (including a fake or two) after being specially asked not to do so by the Lord President of the Council, Lord Salisbury. In March 1859 he returned a stone heavier, gave Mrs Robinson an enamelled chain and got back to work.

Cole's administrative burdens continued to grow. Playfair [28] had returned to Edinburgh just before he was taken ill, and he was left the sole secretary of the department, and so responsible for science in addition to art.

Just before he retired in 1873 Cole said in a speech: 'I have witnessed the conversion of twenty limp Schools of Design into one hundred and twenty flourishing Schools of Art in all parts of the United Kingdom, and other schools like them in the Colonies and the United States'. Cole felt that he had achieved his great Utilitarian aim of bringing art or rather 'elementary drawing', within the reach of every child in the country. Unfortunately, he, like most people at that time, believed that art could be reduced to a set of rules. The curriculum in the art schools, drawn up by Redgrave, was a rigid system of exercises and examinations. Writing some years later, John Ruskin said that: 'the Professorship of Sir Henry Cole at Kensington has corrupted the system of art-teaching all over England into a state of abortion and falsehood from which it will take twenty years to recover'. But Ruskin's voice was not heard by the 'master systematizers' at South Kensington. His lectures and writings influenced intellectuals and those with true artistic tastes, but had no effect on the somewhat philistine politicians and officials who held the public purse-strings.

Charles Dickens found Cole gloriously absurd and introduced him into the second chapter of *Hard Times*, which was serialized in *Household Words* during the summer of 1854. Cole appears as a school inspector: 'A mighty man at cutting and drying, he was; a government officer; in his way (and in most other people's too), a professed pugilist; always in training, always with a system to force down the general throat like a bolus, . . . he had it in charge from high authority to bring about the great public-office Millennium, when Commissioners should reign upon earth'.

Cole, of course, kept going. With the support of Robert Lowe [41], who was Vice-President of the Council, he was wresting money from the government for new buildings and for purchases for the museum's collections. The South Kensington team of Cole, Redgrave, Fowke and the design staff of the museum, spent a great deal of time on the laying out of the Horticultural Gardens on the main square of the Commissioners' estate, [43 & 44], and Cole often had to consult with the Prince Consort at Buckingham Palace, Windsor or Osborne. At the same time he was trying to whip up enthusiasm for the London International Exhibition of 1861, which had to be postponed for a year after the outbreak of the Franco-Austrian War in April 1859. In the end the exhibition was bigger than that of 1851 and more people visited it, but financially it was not a success. The gloom and court mourning following the death of the Prince Consort at the end of 1861 was largely the cause of the failure.

Cole lost his greatest ally and patron in the Prince Consort. But the Prince of Wales [45] was of age, and Cole always had the sympathetic ear of Colonel Grey [46], who had been the Prince Consort's secretary, and who after his death became the Queen's. Money was collected for a memorial to the Prince and Cole hoped that a large concert hall would be part of it. When he saw that there was not going to be one, he set about getting the Royal Albert Hall built [47].

Cole retired in 1873, having served 'Fifty Years of Public Work', as he later called his autobiography. Cobden said to him 'I suppose you will retire into public life'. But Cole did not try to go into Parliament: he became the Managing Director of Scott's Sewage Company.

7   Cole aged 57 in 1865

The company was set up to exploit Scott's patents for turning night soil into manure and cement. Cole hoped that at last he would make a lot of money, but after spending some time living in Birmingham, Manchester and Rochdale [51] to set up treatment plants, there were many difficulties. That at Birmingham was closed as a nuisance, even though in Cole's opinion it smelled of new-baked bread. At another works there was trouble with the machinery. Then it was found that other sewage companies, and there were many, could all too easily infringe Scott's patents and get away with it. The company was wound up in 1879; even the patronage and chairmanship of the Duke of Sutherland [50] could not save it. Cole did not entirely give up, for the Society of Arts continued to offer him a platform for sanitary reform agitation, and he involved the Prince of Wales in a campaign for a better water supply for London. When Cole brought his family back to London, he took a newly-built house in Earl's Court and had the latest model drains put in, ventilated by gas jets that drew off the smells. He sent out cards to everyone he knew, inviting them to call and view the arrangements.

All his life Cole tried to improve the lot of women by finding them professions. His cousins had had to go out as governesses, then the only occupation for middle-class girls who had no money. He had seen the discomfort of their position in an employer's household, awkwardly poised between the family and the servants. Even before he was put in charge of the Schools of Design, he had used women wood-engravers for the illustrations to *The Home Treasury*. At the Schools he tried to train girls as artists and engravers, but men did not want girls working for them in their studios. As soon as he retired, he tried again.

Starting with a committee at the Society of Arts and continuing under the patronage of the Duke of Edinburgh (Queen Victoria's second son), he set up the National Training School for Music. The Queen, the Prince of Wales, the Duke of Edinburgh, and the Society of Arts itself, all promised to fund scholarships, so that students from all over the country might train as teachers of music. The Commissioners leased a site just west of the Albert Hall, and the building was designed, in a curious half-eastern style, by Cole's eldest son, Lieut H H Cole RE. He, at that time, happened to be on leave from India, where he was Superintendent of the Archaeological Survey in the North-West Provinces. The school opened in 1876, with Arthur Sullivan as principal, and Charlotte Thompson, by then a widow, as house-keeper. Alan Cole, another of Cole's sons, was the honorary secretary. In 1882 the school closed, to make way for the founding of the Royal College of Music. The building is now the Royal College of Organists.

Cole had another success with his National Training School for Cookery. Once again the Society of Arts helped, and the chairman was Frederick Leveson-Gower [52]. One of Cole's daughters, Rose, wrote a cookery book, and the pupils, carefully segregated, ranged from Lady Florence Gower, a daughter of the Duke of Sutherland, to domestic servants paid for by their employers.

The pace of his life gradually told on Cole. His heart had begun to beat irregularly when he was in his fifties and at seventy-three he was worn out. He died on 18 April 1882 at his house in London, with his family at his bedside.

He was made a Companion of the Bath for his work on the Great Exhibition, but his knighthood was delayed until 1875. In 1871, the Society of Arts gave him the Albert Medal. He was given the Legion of Honour in 1855, and promoted to a higher grade in 1867.

Ruskin's twenty years soon passed by, and when the Arts and Crafts Movement brought about a change in art-teaching Cole's framework of schools and government grants did at least mean that the new, more relaxed methods of teaching could reach the whole country. At South Kensington, the Royal College of Art, the Royal College of Music, the Imperial College of Science and Technology and the Science Museum are still close to his museum and the Royal Albert Hall.

Sir Henry Trueman Wood should have the last word with a quotation taken from his letter of 1909, mentioned at the beginning of this essay:

> Most of those who knew Henry Cole are dead, but to the few who still live and remember that strenuous official it seems a little hard that *The Times* should publish an account of the museum which he originated without a word of reference to its virtual founder. It is only 27 years since he died. In his day he had a great reputation. He served his country earnestly and well for 50 years. . . . Probably he would not have greatly cared. As he was indifferent to personal credit, he probably would not have specially desired posthumous fame. He liked his own way, and he generally got it, though his methods were not such as endeared him either to the superiors whose orders he evaded or to the subordinates whose submission he compelled. He had many really great and many extremely disagreeable qualities. He was quite impervious to ridicule, and would collect and chuckle over the numerous caricatures of which 'Cole, CB' was the frequent object. He did more than any other single man to bring about the modern change of sentiment in the appreciation of industrial art, and this though he had no aesthetic judgment and no artistic power. Within his limits he was a great man, and his work deserves, especially at this moment, at least the tribute of recognition.

The Illustrations

1 The Writing School at Christ's Hospital

When Henry was sent to Christ's Hospital at the age of eleven, it was still in its old monastic buildings in the City of London, with some later buildings added, such as the Writing School shown here. The school had been founded by Edward VI as a charity school and the boys wore, and wear to this day, a Tudor uniform of blue coat and yellow stockings. Anachronistic knickerbockers were added in 1810. The Cole family had a right to places in the school because an ancestor had bequeathed his estate to the school to endow two scholarships for his descendants.

Sixty years after his time at school, Cole wrote down some of his memories. The boys slept in wooden cubicles, like monks' cells. They got up at six in summer and seven in winter. 'The washing and kindred arrangements were simply beastly. Forty boys used to scramble to wash their hands and feet in one large tub fighting over a towel to dry themselves.' The food was very poor and the boys were fed mainly on bread and the cheapest and thinnest sort of beer, which they called 'swipes'. They were given boiled meat twice a week; the mutton on Fridays they nicknamed 'gags', it was so tough. But '. . . hungry as we were the boys were healthy – and the death rate was not high.'

Writing lessons were compulsory for all the six hundred boys. Mathematics were taught only to boys who were going to sea. Greek and Latin were taught, but out of grammar books written in Latin. Cole wrote that 'by dint of ceaseless gabbling . . . I got the sounds more or less by heart'. Canings and floggings occurred daily and some of the masters gave them for fun. All the masters were clergymen. Bullying, particularly by the 'Sea' boys, made life a misery for those who were small. 'When I left school and for years afterwards I looked back upon it as a place where all my time had been wasted, and where I had learnt worse than nothing. . . . I spelt badly, read stammeringly, wrote well.' He won a silver medal for his writing. 'I could repeat a few Latin scraps and this certainly helped me to copy the mediaeval Latin jargon of the public records when that became my occupation.'

1

2 Sir Francis Palgrave (1788–1861)

Cole wrote: 'I took off my Tudor dress on the 9th April 1823 and on the 10th presented myself in an Oxford mixture suit with tailed coat at Mr Cohen's office.'

Francis Ephraim Cohen was the son of a Jewish stockbroker, but had been baptised a Christian in 1821, perhaps in order to be able to be called to the Bar. In October 1823 he married Elizabeth Turner, who drew the sketch of him shown here. She came from a prominent East Anglian family and Mr Cohen adopted her mother's maiden name of Palgrave. The Turners were a remarkable family: they were rich, civilised and artistic. Following their example, Cole learnt perspective drawing from Charles Wild and water-colour painting from David Cox. He played the flute and sang and had dancing lessons from a 'hop merchant'.

Mr Palgrave had chosen Henry and two other 'Blues' for their neat handwriting to copy out old documents so that they could be prepared for publication by the Record Commission. His task, which he had thought of for himself and had had approved by the Commission, was to edit and publish a large collection of medieval parliamentary writs. He was paid more than anyone else working for the Commission, and received over £6,000 in five years for work that was mostly done for him by boy-clerks like Henry, to whom he paid £60 a year. He was not doing anything out of the ordinary in making use of the Commission in this way. Patronage, or 'jobbery' as those who disapproved called it, was the only way of getting any employment at the time. The peers, politicians and prelates who made up the Commission were content to spend £10,000 a year on helping their friends and few of them were interested in the records themselves. In any case, the Commission had no say in how the records were stored. They were kept in over fifty different places around London, and all that could be done was to pull out a few from the heap, transcribe and publish them. Palgrave was a good lawyer and a considerable scholar, taking a special interest in the middle ages and therefore in the ancient records. His father-in-law wrote of his 'extraordinary depth & variety of his knowledge & accuracy of his judgement'. Another friend remembered his 'air of high breeding and the show of natural dignity that are sometimes observable in Jews of the highest type and finest quality'. A most loving man in his private life, it has to be said that he was over-greedy for money in his career. From 1834 he had two supposedly full-time appointments, that of Keeper of the Records at the Chapter House, Westminster, and that of Commissioner of the Municipal Corporations. He was knighted for his drafting of the Municipal Corporations Bill. His 'jobbery' was made public by the report of the Select Committee, and Palgrave was so incensed that he accused the Committee of libel. However, he was appointed Deputy Keeper of the Public Records, a post he held up to his death.

---

3 'See the Conquering hero (heroine) Comes'

This sketch is of Henry, aged twenty-one, dressed up as a chaperone at a New Years Eve party in

London in 1830. He wrote in his diary: 'Accompanied Miss Darby as her Aunt to Mrs Hughes without being discovered, although suspicion was resting strongly upon me.'

The Hughes family were old friends of the Coles, and lived in Gower Street. There were three daughters, Maria, Emma and Elizabeth. This sketch is likely to be by Emma, and Cole may have kept it because he was in love with her. He proposed and was rejected on her behalf by Mrs Hughes about twelve months later.

Miss Darby was a friend of the Hughes's, whom Cole had first met a few weeks before. She was able to introduce him to Geraldine Jewsbury, Mrs Carlyle's close friend.

4 Thomas Love Peacock (1785–1866)

Novelist, critic, satirist, poet, wit, devoted friend of Shelley and official of the East India Company, Peacock had a profound influence on young Henry Cole's career. They met in the Spring of 1826, when the Cole family rented part of Peacock's house in Blackfriars, after he had decided to move his family outside London. He took an immediate fancy to Henry, then aged nearly 22, and introduced him to 'the disquisitive set of young men' headed by John Stuart Mill. He thus put Cole in touch with the young politicians and political thinkers who were foremost in the agitation that led up to the Reform Bill of 1832.

Peacock encouraged Henry in his desire to be a journalist by getting him to 'devil' his music and theatre criticisms when he was out of London and not able to do them. Cole published his own first notice, a review of Malibran in *Cenerentola*, in *The Globe* in April 1830, and followed it a few months later with an article about the Tower of London in *The Examiner*. Peacock allowed Cole to be the first to publish some of his 'Paper Money Lyrics', which he did in 1837 in his own newspaper *The Guide*.

This photograph of Peacock is the frontispiece to his collected works that Cole edited in 1875. Though taken when he was over seventy, in 1857, it gives a good idea of the kind of man he was: 'a kind-hearted, genial, friendly man, who loved to share his enjoyment of life with all around him, and self-indulgent without being selfish'.

4

5 John Stuart Mill (1806–1873)

Carlyle first met this great philosopher and political economist in 1830, when Mill was 24. He immediately wrote to his wife:

A slender rather tall and elegant youth with small clear Roman-nosed face, two small earnestly smiling eyes; modest, remarkably gifted with precision of utterance, enthusiastic, yet lucid, calm: not a great, yet a distinctly gifted and amiable youth. We had almost four hours of the best talk I have mingled in for long.

Cole and Mill were friends for many years. Introduced to him by Peacock [4] in 1826, Cole was immediately welcomed into the charmed circle of young men that surrounded Mill. Within a few days Cole was going to early morning classes at the house of George Grote, and attending lectures in the evenings. At weekends they walked immense distances in the country round London, 'talking and laughing the whole way'. The band included such men as Horace Grant, Edwin Chadwick, John Roebuck, John Graham and John Sterling. Cole joined Mill's Debating Society and listened to young radicals making speeches on how they would set the world to rights. They wanted universal suffrage and a secret ballot at a time when the idea of giving even male house-owners the vote was thought to be dangerously democratic.

5

of people who called on them in their rooms at India House. For years Cole saw Mill almost every day, often walking with him from Kensington into the City, and Mill was always generous in his support of Cole's projects and struggles. The clever, busy, practical Cole would seem an unlikely intimate for a brilliant, over-educated, contemplative young man like John Mill, particularly since Mill, at the time they first met in 1826, was so depressed that he thought of committing suicide. It may be that in some way they complemented each other. They gradually drifted apart, and met less and less, especially after Mill began to spend half of the year in France. His sister Harriet remained a friend of the Cole family to the end of her life.

6 Sir William Molesworth (1810–1855)

This rich, dashing duel-fighting young baronet became Member of Parliament for East Cornwall in 1833. A close friend of Charles Buller, he was a Philosophic Radical, as the Utilitarians were known in Parliament, and was quickly introduced to John Mill by George Grote. Grote's wife, the redoutable Harriet, said that when she first met Sir William he had 'a pleasant countenance, expressive blue eyes, florid complexion, and light brown hair; a slim and neatly made figure, about 5 ft. 10 in. in height, with small, well-shaped hands and feet.' Carlyle met him at Charles Buller's house and noticed that he was 'a vehement smoker of tobacco!'

Molesworth shared a house in Eaton Square with another rich young politician, John Temple Leader, where they gave dinner parties to their Radical friends. In 1836 they founded the Reform Club as a meeting place for Radicals and Whigs. Cole joined immediately and dined there almost every day 'off 2 mutton chops & a pint of porter'.

John Mill and his friends felt they should have a magazine to help hold the Radical party together, and to shape opinion in and out of Parliament. Molesworth agreed to put up the money and *The London Review* first came out in April 1835, owned and edited by him, but really controlled by John Mill from his room at India House. It was a quarterly and started well with James Mill, Charles Buller, Thomas Love Peacock, George Grote and John Mill contributing, but it always lost money. Molesworth also bought up *The Westminster Review*, so that by the end of 1837 he had spent over £2,000. He gave the combined magazine, known as *The London and Westminster Review*, to John Mill. Each issue cost Mill £100, and about a year later he handed it over to Cole and William Hickson. Hickson, a rich shoe manufacturer, edited

They were followers of Jeremy Bentham and his friend, James Mill, the father of John. They were 'Benthamites' or 'Utilitarians', and to put it at its very simplest, they believed in 'the greatest good for the greatest number'. Only what was useful was thought to be beneficial, and over the next fifty years many of those who strove to achieve reforms that affected the 'people'—a Benthamite concept— such as education or public health, were Utilitarians who had fallen under the spell of the younger Mill.

In January 1829, John Mill alienated many of his Utilitarian friends at the Debating Society by making a two-hour speech in praise of Wordsworth's poetry. Romance had no place in the Benthamite creed. Cole hoped to make a speech in reply at a succeeding meeting, but even though Mill lent him the notes for his own speech, he found himself out of his depth and admitted that he was not up to it. However, when Mill visited Wordsworth in the Lake District in the Summer of 1831, Cole joined him for part of his walking tour. A year later they went together on a walking and sketching holiday to the Isle of Wight and the New Forest.

Mill worked at the East India House, as did his father. Being officials, they could not be Members of Parliament, or be seen to be active in politics in any way. They exerted their influence through their writings and through the enormous number

EDITOR OF LONDON & WESTMINSTER REVIEW.

the *Review* for ten years, but Cole had to withdraw after two issues.

Sir William Molesworth continued in Parliament, voting with Grote in favour of the secret ballot and working for reforms in the administration of the new colonies in Australia. He was appointed Colonial Secretary a few months before his death.

humour and exquisite delicacy' that he 'enchanted the House', and the Committee was granted. Buller chaired the Committee and Cole coached the witnesses and appeared as one himself. Cole drafted the Committee's Report and Buller nicknamed him the 'attorney for the prosecution'.

After the report was published they joined with other radicals to run a weekly newspaper *The Guide*, which for 3d was to provide 'really useful intelligence' of births, deaths, marriages and market reports gathered from all over the country. It only ran for eight issues before they abandoned it.

In the Spring of 1838 Buller went to Canada as chief secretary to Lord Durham – 'Radical Jack – and he asked Cole to go with him. Cole declined, partly because he saw a chance of working again in the Public Records, and partly because Marian was expecting their second child.

After the failure of the Durham Mission, Buller returned to Parliament and was able to use his influence to help Cole with the penny postage; and he spoke several times in the House of Commons about the new Public Record Office. Unhappily, he died tragically early, aged only forty-two, as the result of an operation. His mother died of a broken heart three months later.

7 Charles Buller (1806–1848)

Carlyle, who had been his tutor, called Buller 'the genialist radical I have ever met'. He was six feet three inches tall, and in spite of a broken nose, extremely handsome. He inherited his great charm from his mother, whom he adored. He arrived in London in 1828 with a reputation as a speaker in the Cambridge Union, and just a year later became a Member of Parliament for one of the rotten boroughs that his family controlled in Cornwall. Cole first met him in John Mill's room at the India House in July 1830, though he had often heard him speak at the London Debating Society.

Buller's speeches were always brilliant, but he was so often carried away by his own wit and made so many jokes, that he was not taken seriously. While he could work very hard, he was often lazy, perhaps partly because he never had good health. Mill said of him that he had energy but 'no persevering industry'. In the House of Commons Buller spoke mainly on colonisation and had a part in founding the South Australia Company. He always had time to listen to Cole's accounts of the enormities of the Record Commission and its secretary, and after Cole was dismissed in November 1835 he agreed to ask for a Select Committee. Cole said that his speech was so full of 'wit and

7

8 Lord Langdale (1783–1851)

After the disclosures made in the Select Committee report, the Government could no longer trust the Record Commission, but it was saved from the embarrassment of doing anything by the death of William IV in 1837, when the Commission automatically lapsed. The care of the records was then given to Lord Langdale, the Master of the Rolls. As Henry Bickersteth, he had trained as a doctor and had not turned to the Law until he was nearly thirty. Then he had a most successful career at the Bar, culminating in January 1836 when he was made Master of the Rolls, a Privy Councillor and a baron. He had been a friend of Jeremy Bentham, and was a staunch Utilitarian. James Mill recommended Cole to him, and Charles Buller persuaded him to reinstate Cole.

Lord Langdale put Cole in charge of the records of the Exchequer of Pleas, with an office in a house in Whitehall Yard, close to the Banqueting House. In 1841, Cole moved across Trafalgar Square to the old riding school of Carlton House. Here many records were collected from the smaller depositories and Cole's 'staff of twenty and more workmen of the bookbinding class' cleaned, repaired and catalogued them. Cole invented a method of colour-coding the records from the different courts of law. This work was done in preparation for the move into a proper record office. Lord Langdale came to be known as 'the father of the records' for his repeated efforts, in and out of the House of Lords, to persuade the Government to build a central record depository. It was not until 1850 that it was decided to build it in Chancery Lane, and the foundation stone was laid in May 1851, five weeks after his death from overwork.

Cole wrote of Lord Langdale: 'Although my official superior, for more than ten years, he always treated me as a friend.' He understood Cole and gave him good advice, which Cole noted in his diary, but was incapable of acting on. When they had only known each other a few months, Lord Langdale was 'counselling against too rough & direct bearing & that diplomacy was always necessary to effect objects. He said my character was always to give people pokes & that it was too critical. For his own part he did not mind it, but the world in general disliked it.'

He approved of Cole's work in the campaign for the penny post, a reform dear to any Utilitarian's heart, but he was less sure about Cole's journalism and cautioned him about it. He was 'pained' when Cole had leave of absence from the record service to work on the Great Exhibition, indeed he was so saddened that he could hardly bring himself to

8

shake hands with him; but he took the trouble to call at the Treasury to make sure that Cole was paid his salary.

9 Henry and Marian Cole in 1855

This photograph was taken in Paris in 1855, almost certainly by Thurston Thompson. Cole is wearing his uniform of a civil Companion of the Bath.

Henry and Marian were first cousins. Their mothers were sisters, and Marian's mother, Mrs Bond, lived near her other married sister, Mrs Webb, at Epping. As a young man, Henry often walked the twenty-odd miles to visit the two families of cousins. He would leave London on Saturday afternoon, and get up at five on Monday morning in order to reach his office by ten. Marian went as a governess to the Maitlands, who lived at Loughton Hall, not far from Epping. When Cole met them, he wrote: 'Introduced to Mr & Mrs M. The first a hasty bluff good humoured, not very cultivated or informed person. A modern specimen of antient John Bull, hating the French, Up for the King & so forth. Mrs M: pleasant in face & manner.'

There are no signs in the Cole family papers that Henry and Marian ever fell romantically in love. It is true that they were married in secret at

19

St Martin's-in-the-Fields at the end of December 1833, but after two days, they were able to part without much sorrow, and Marian went back to the Maitlands. There are hints that there was family opposition to the marriage, perhaps because Cole's income was only £150 a year. In the following April Marian came to live with Henry in his rooms at the top of a house in the Adelphi.

Cole cannot have been an easy man to be married to. His constant activity must have been exhausting. Marian played little part in his public life. When he dined with Lord Granville or stayed with the Prince of Wales he went alone. His diary shows that when he was at home he usually worked, or if he did relax enough to play a game of cards, he did so in a competitive spirit, even when playing against his children. He noted in his diary whether he lost or won. Marian never had the usual comforts of a well-to-do Victorian family. There was never enough money for a carriage, and her domestic staff never included a footman or a lady's maid. As she grew older she took on a hardened, pent-up look, though the very small number of her letters that survive are full of gaiety and charm.

9

10

10 Cole and his wife and their eight children in 1858

Henrietta and Laetitia, the two oldest girls, are on the left. Behind Tishy is Harry, who spent most of his career in India, where as a Royal Engineer he surveyed historic buildings. Mary rests her hand on his shoulder. She married (Sir) George Bartley, M.P., the founder of the National Penny Bank, who was Assistant Director of the Science Division in Cole's department. Sitting low on the ground is Isabella, who married Frank Fowke; next is Rose, who after falling in love with a man who had no money, became a missionary. Granville leans against his father, and Alan is on the other side of Marian. Alan was the one of the children who remained most closely linked with the museum, becoming an Assistant Secretary in the department. He was an expert on textiles, particularly on lace.

Cole was not at all what we think of as a typical Victoria father. His diary never mentions that he ever punished his children, it rather records his enjoyment of them. He nursed them for whole evenings when they were babies, played with them when they grew older, recorded their childish sayings and took them about with him whenever he could.

11 Rowland Hill (1795–1879)

The inventor of the prepaid penny post stands beside his desk on which are reminders of his great work: the postage cover [13], a letter with a penny black stamp on it and a calendar showing the day of its first use, 24 May (1840). It seems to us now so logical that the sender of a letter should pay for it, that it is hard to understand what a revolutionary idea it was. Until 1840 the recipient had to pay the cost of postage, which was calculated on the number of sheets in the letter, and on the distance it was carried. The average cost for a letter was 9d. When Hill suggested a flat rate of 1d for any letter weighing under half an ounce, carried any distance, it was greeted with ridicule.

In the Spring of 1837 Hill published his pamphlet on his scheme, and as Cole wanted to review it in *The Guide*, he called on him to discuss it. Hill at that time was the Secretary of the South Australian Commission, which was reforming the way land was granted to immigrants in the new colonies. Molesworth [6], Buller [7] and other Philosophic Radicals were Commissioners. Hill was a Utilitarian: his family ran a famous school, and its advanced teaching methods had been approved of by Jeremy Bentham.

In February 1838, Hill asked Cole to help him and introduced him to a pressure group of London city merchants, who had formed themselves into the Mercantile Committee to campaign for a more efficient postal system. With Lord Langdale's permission, Cole became the secretary and used the experience gained in the battle over the public records to good effect. Hill said of him: 'He was the author of almost innumerable devices, by which in his indefatigable ingenuity he contrived to draw public attention to the proposed measure.' The most interesting of these was his weekly newspaper *The Post Circular or Weekly Advocate for a Cheap, Swift & Sure Postage*. Newspapers were carried free by the Post Office, so Cole could distribute news, notices of meetings, forms of petitions to both Houses of Parliament and so on, all over the country for the cost of printing only. Generally about 1700 copies of the *Post Circular* were sent out each week, so that the Post Office was forced to carry the propaganda for its own reform. Cole wrote most of *The Circular* and edited it, and himself drew the cartoon of the mail coach [12].

He wrote a little play in which the Queen was imagined discussing the penny post with her ministers at Windsor, and pronounced herself wholly in favour of it. 100,000 copies were sold, and

11

Dickens's publishers, Chapman and Hall, bound a further 40,000 into one of the monthly parts of *Nicholas Nickleby*.

At long last, in the summer of 1839, the Government finally gave in and passed a bill to introduce the penny post, and in October Cole began to work after office hours with Rowland Hill to organise the working and introduction of the scheme. Cole's knowledge of printing and engraving was useful when it became necessary to produce stamps that would be difficult to forge, and he was put in charge of finding a design for the postage cover that was to be used before the introduction of stamps [13].

Hill got little thanks from the Government for all he had done and it was nearly twenty years before he was knighted. The Society of Arts, however, took the first opportunity to give him its highest award, and gave him its Albert Medal in 1864, the first year in which it was presented.

Though Cole and Hill worked closely together for several years, they never really liked each other. Cole thought Hill could not get on with people.

When he read Hill's biography he said it was 'correct, impassive, foggy like himself'.

12 The Edinburgh Mail

This wood-engraving after a drawing by Cole was published in *The Post Circular* at the end of April 1839. It explains what proportion of the mail was carried free by the Post Office. It includes nearly five hundred letters 'franked' by peers or Members of Parliament for themselves or their friends: this was a privilege that was much abused. The original caption to the cartoon reads:

This Sketch—an exact representation of the contents of the Edinburgh Mail on the 2d March, 1838—has been designed for the particular instruction of the Postmaster-general, who, notwithstanding he stands at the head of the Post-Office class, has shown that he is at the bottom of it, in respect of knowledge of the rudiments of his business.

12

13 The Postage Cover

It was planned to introduce the prepaid penny post on 10 January 1840. Towards the end of 1839, the idea of a specially designed postage cover was mooted. Cole was sent to call on several Royal Academicians, but it was the new Chancellor of the Exchequer, Sir Francis Baring, who suggested William Mulready [14]. Cole called on him, and found him 'very intelligent and affable'; he 'appeared readily to enter into the idea & agreed to make a trial'. When Cole first saw the design, he called it 'highly poetic'. The Council of the Royal Academy also liked it, but everyone else thought it was ridiculous, particularly as a leg was left off one of the angels, which no-one noticed, not

Cole, not John Thompson, who did the engraving, not even Mulready himself.

Considering the design many years later, Cole thought it was more suitable for a fresco: 'The postage cover was for dry commercial use, in which sentiment had no part. . . . I now think that everything, even a mere meaningless ornamental design, would have been out of place.'

The example of the cover that is shown below is a proof copy. The cover was not issued until April 1840, when it was printed in blue. It was a convenient way for businesses to prepay postage in bulk, and most of them had the inside of the cover filled with advertisements.

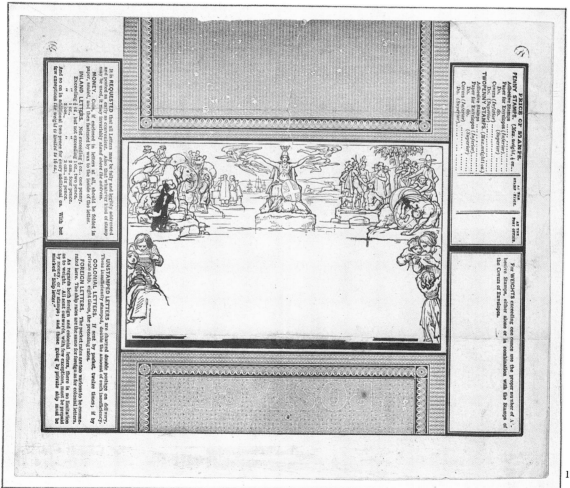

13

14 William Mulready (1786–1863)

William Mulready was an Irishman, with a generous, wild, passionate side to his nature, that was quite at odds with the pernickety way in which he finished his paintings. He was born in County Clare, the stoniest and poorest county in the West. His family moved to London when he was still very small and he began his career by selling drawings to his friends at school. At fourteen he became a student at the Royal Academy Schools, and two years later won a prize given by the Society of Arts. He made friends with John Varley, the watercolourist, and went to live in his house and help him with his pupils. Unfortunately, he fell in love with one of Varley's sisters and married her when he was just seventeen and she a year older. To support himself, Mulready gave lessons and illustrated children's books. He was unable to make enough, and said that he remembered 'the time when I had a wife, four children, nothing to do, and was 600*l*. in debt'. He had a roaring temper and a taste for bad company, and would bring home prize fighters to the house. Though extreme poverty contributed to the breakup of his marriage, it was Mulready's temper and violence that caused his wife to leave him in 1809.

In 1839, when Cole first met him, he was at the peak of his career, a regular exhibitor at the Royal Academy for over thirty years and an Academician for more than twenty. His paintings and drawings were bought by fashionable collectors from the Queen downwards. She particularly admired his drawings of the nude figure. Mulready introduced Cole to his close friend John Linnell, who had painted this splendid portrait in 1833. Cole was also introduced to John Sheepshanks, Mulready's principal patron, who later gave his collection of English paintings to the museum.

Cole liked Mulready as a man, and admired his work enormously. In 1848, he arranged a loan exhibition of his work at the Society of Arts. Mulready encouraged Cole to write books for children and illustrated one of them. He allowed one of his paintings to be reproduced on a *Felix Summerly* vase, and he helped Cole when he was writing a catalogue to the National Gallery and gave up two evenings to help him correct it. After Mulready's death, Cole held a large retrospective exhibition at the South Kensington Museum.

In 1876, James McNeill Whistler invited Sir Henry and Alan Cole to view the Peacock Room. Alan wrote in his diary: 'Jimmy much disgusted at my father's telling him that, in taking so much pains over his work, and in the minuteness of his etched work, he really was like Mulready, who was equally scrupulous.'

14

15

24

15 Maria Callcott (1785–1842)

Lady Callcott was the wife of the painter Sir Augustus Callcott. Cole only knew her during the last two years of her life, when she was over fifty and bedridden and could no longer have looked as she did when Sir Thomas Lawrence painted her as a young and beautiful woman. She had been in India and to South America, and had written accounts of her travels. She also wrote children's books, of which the best known is *Little Arthur's History of England*, published in 1835. Cole was greatly charmed by her and wrote more about her in his diary than he did about any other person.

When he met her in February 1841 he wrote: 'Though an invalid she brightens up with life & vigour & says many sharp good things, loves Art, Children & seems thoroughly to enjoy every thing that has good in it.' Two days later she talked to him 'about Giotto, The Sisteen Chapel: Good dinners, Nursery Rhymes &c.' And again a month later: 'I like the fine hearty sense of truth in her, & the absence of all humbug'.

Cole began to call on her almost every Sunday, taking one of his little daughters with him. She suggested that he should write books for his children, and he helped her last book *The Bracken-burners, and little Mary's Four Saturdays* through the press.

Sir Augustus and Lady Callcott had married late in life and had no children, but they had a wide circle of young relations. Sir Augustus's niece was the wife of a composer, William Horsley, and was the mother of Cole's painter friend, J C Horsley. One of her daughters married I K Brunel, the famous engineer, and another married Cole's cousin John Bond. J C Horsley's second wife was the sister of Seymour Haden. Cole came to know them all.

16 The Felix Summerly Christmas Card

This is the first Christmas Card ever to be published. It was drawn for Cole in November 1843 by his friend John Horsley, and published by the Felix Summerly Home Treasury in time for Christmas. No-one knows what gave Cole the idea to publish the card, but it seems logical to think that people might want to send cards to their friends once the cost of sending one was reduced to 1d. It may be that Cole had seen some of the general-purpose greeting cards that had been published from time

To

A MERRY CHRISTMAS
AND
A HAPPY NEW YEAR
TO YOU

Published at Summerly's Home Treasury Office.
12 Old Bond Street London.   From   16

25

to time. His friend John Thompson had engraved one as long ago as 1829. It is curious that Cole, in his diary, refers to the card as a 'remembrance' or 'congratulation' card. The phrase 'Christmas card' seems to have come in later on.

Cole's card, lithographed and hand-coloured, cost 1/–, which seems a very high price, when one knows that Cole generally paid that much for his dinner at the Reform Club. The card was sold by Cole's new friend and publisher, Joseph Cundall, from his shop in Bond Street.

Cole's innovation started a trend which grew into an industry. Towards the end of the century Raphael Tuck re-issued the card, machine-coloured, for only 2d. It has been reprinted many times since.

17   Richard Redgrave (1804–1888)

For more than forty years Richard Redgrave was Cole's most loving and biddable friend and colleague. They became friends in 1841, joined forces to improve the Schools of Design and were appointed together, eleven years later, to the Department of Practical Art. Redgrave, who was a painter, designed the prettiest of Felix Summerly's Art-Manufactures, and illustrated some of the Home

17

Treasury books. He began to teach at the School of Design in 1847, and was made headmaster in 1849.

When Mr Labouchere in 1852 offered Redgrave, by then an R A, the part-time post of Art-Superintendent, he asked him if he could work with Cole, and Redgrave assured him that he thought he could. Cole too, had 'rather objected', as he put it, to 'shared responsibility'. However, the two got on well, as Redgrave was content to be the subordinate. From time to time, though, there are hints of rebellion in his journal, when he says that he knows he will never get his due credit for such successes as the Sheepshanks and Ellison gifts of pictures to the museum, or for his invention of the rules and examinations for the Schools of Art.

Cole had a habit of teasing Redgrave, using the same joke over and over again. He would present him to the King of the Belgians, or some other distinguished visitor to the museum, as the Pope of South Kensington, because he was *infallible* in Art! There was always a laugh and Redgrave became thoroughly sick of it. He was a most reluctant civil servant. One can only assume that he needed the money, as he lacked the Utilitarian reforming zeal that drove Cole on. All he wanted to do was paint, and his happiest times were spent with his wife and children at their country house at Abinger Common, only about four miles from Shere where the Cole family had their cottage [38]. The two families often went on expeditions and picnics together during their summer holidays. In 1858 when Cole was told that he had to go to Italy for his health, Redgrave and one of his brothers went with him for part of the time.

At Cole's suggestion, Redgrave was made Surveyor of the Queen's Pictures in 1857, but when the Queen offered him a knighthood twelve years later, he was too modest to accept it. He worked on in the department as Director of the Art Division for some years after Cole retired, and did not leave until he was nearly seventy-two. He was succeeded by Edward Poynter, the painter who was to become President of the Royal Academy and a baronet. At Redgrave's last prize-giving Poynter paid tribute to him: 'Mr Redgrave is the author of the most perfect system of national art instruction ever devised—a system which is unique in Europe, and the value of which has been recognised in many countries.'

Towards the end of his life Redgrave became nearly blind, with cataracts in both eyes. Cole invited him to a firework party in 1881 and seemed surprised that he went home early.

This touching little self-portrait, measuring only 6×7 inches, shows Redgrave as quite a young man, before he met Cole.

18

18a   John Bell (1811–1895)

Bell was a successful sculptor, and he and Cole met in the 1840s, when Cole was forming lifelong friendships with so many artists. One of Bell's statues, 'Dorothea', was produced, at reduced size, as a parian ornament and became the only really popular Art-Manufacture. Bell was a loyal follower of Cole at the Society of Arts, but though they met almost weekly over many years, Cole never gives any opinion of him in his diary. It may be that he was a bore.

Bell came from East Anglia, where he began his career as a boy, carving gravestones. Then he went to the Royal Academy Schools in London, and won a prize given by the Society of Arts. At the Royal Academy Exhibition of 1841, he exhibited 'The Eagle Shooter' which became known as 'The Eagle Slayer' and was a sensation at the Great Exhibition, where it was shown under a cast iron canopy. It now stands outside the Bethnal Green Museum. In 1842 a magazine wrote of him: 'His mind is deeply imbued with poetic feeling; he is one of the few artists who attempt higher efforts than mere busts; and as his success has been great, he may take a very prominent station in the most elevated department of the arts. We consider his onward and upward career as matter of certainty.' Bell was the first artist whom Cole approached for his Felix Summerly Art-Manufactures [25]. He designed the

'Brides Inkstand', which was published in 1847. It was not a commercial success, though one was bought by the Queen. 'Dorothea' came out a year later, and sold so well that it often had to be re-ordered from Mintons when stocks ran out. Nowadays, it is the Art-Manufacture most often found in antique shops. In 1848 Bell made an important contribution to the furnishing of houses all over the English-speaking world by designing a bread board [18b]. It was of lime wood, with a circle of carved wheat, rye, barley and oats at its edge. In 1880, Cole wrote of it that it 'revived the use of wooden bread platters or trenchers. . . . From the years 1848 to the present time, the Summerly platter has been sold – besides innumerable other versions produced at the lowest possible prices; in fact, a new branch of industry was established at Sheffield, and, being easy of manufacture, at places more or less throughout the Kingdom.'

Unlike most of Cole's friends, Bell never held an official position. His sentimental figures exactly caught the mood of mid-Victorian taste and he was never without commissions. However, his great wish was to put up an obelisk, and he came forward with a design whenever any monument was projected. The only one that he was allowed to design was a memorial to Cole's colleague at the Great Exhibition, Sir William Reid, and that was in Bermuda. His idea for the Albert Memorial was turned down, though he did do 'America' one of the large groups that represent the four continents, at the corners of the base of the memorial when it was built.

By the 1870s, Bell had lost his popularity with the public; his sugary statues of naked babies and young women were no longer admired. Nor did he receive much recognition from his fellow artists and was not elected an Academician. After his death one obituary spoke of him as an artist 'whose successful career was a matter of surprise to himself as much as to others'.

THE BREAD PLATTER.   18b

27

19

19 ' "Come let's to bed" says Sleepy-head '

'Come, let's to bed' says Sleepy-head.
'Let's stay awhile,' says Slow:
'Put on the pot' says Greedy-sot,
'We'll sup before we go.'

This rhyme is taken from *Traditional Nursery Songs of England*, the first of the *Home Treasury* series of children's books that Cole published. It was an immediate success, with over 800 subscribed for before publication. Just after it first appeared in May 1843, John Mill told Cole that 'Felix Summerly would be as notorious as the brothers Grimm'.

Cole's contribution to children's literature lay in the fact that he made nursery rhymes and folk tales respectable. He brought the oral tradition from the kitchen into the parlour. His books were small and intended for children to handle; they were beautifully produced, printed in the newly-revived Caslon typeface, and bound by Charles Whittingham. The publisher was Joseph Cundall, who became Cole's close friend. The illustrations were mostly by living Royal Academicians – this one is by John Linnell – though some books had engravings after classic painters – Titian, Durer, Botticelli and Rembrandt.

20 William Makepeace Thackeray (1811–1863)

In the 1850s Cole and Thackeray lived opposite one another in Onslow Square, South Kensington. Their friendship was of that casual, neighbourly sort that leaves no written record. Cole first mentions Thackeray in his diary in 1837, but it is hard to believe that they had not met before, as they were both friends of Charles Buller [7] and William Molesworth, [6].

In 1839, when the campaign to repeal the Corn Laws was at its height, Richard Cobden asked Cole to help *The Anti-Corn-Law Circular*, which had been started in imitation of *The Post Circular*. Cole was too busy, but suggested that Thackeray might be asked to do some cartoons, which he did. Cole wrote to Cobden: 'The artist is a genius, both with his pencil and with his pen. His vocation is literary. He is full of humour and feeling.'

Cole recognised Thackeray's talents, but it was not for another ten years that *Vanity Fair* was published and the general public accorded him his place as one of the great novelists of the English language.

Thackeray, who enjoyed gambling occasionally, lost £500 in an unlucky speculation in a railway company. Cole brought him into the railway gauge disputes and he wrote two Jeames Yellowplush letters to *Punch* about how Jeames and his wife, Mary Hann lost their baby, Michael Hangelo, in the flurry of changing from Brunel's wide gauge, to the narrower one at Gloucester.

This drawing of Thackeray shows him a few years before he met Cole. It is by Daniel Maclise, a well-known painter, who designed for Cole's Art-Manufactures.

20

Thackeray's wife was a depressive and unable to live with her family, and so his two little girls were brought up by his mother in Paris. In the 1870s, the elder of them, Anny, wrote an account of her childhood for her niece, Laura Stephen. In it she says:

> One of the nicest things that ever happened to us when we were children in Paris was the arrival of a huge parcel, wh my Grannie cut open and inside there were piles & piles of the most beautiful delightful wonderful fairy tale books all painted with pictures – I thought they would never come to an end, but alas! in a week we had read them all. They were called the Felix Summerly Series & on the first page was written – To my three daughters Laetitia Henrietta & Mary I dedicate these volumes. I used to think that they must be the happiest little girls in the world but I never thought that we should ever know them.

In fact, as soon as the younger girl, Minny, was six years old, their father brought them to live with him in Kensington. The Coles lived only a short distance away and the children became friends; the friendship was reinforced when they all lived in Onslow Square.

In 1860, Thackeray was planning a new magazine, *The Cornhill*, and Cole got the cover designed by Godfrey Sykes, a young artist who worked at the museum. Cole and a number of his colleagues were contributors to *The Cornhill*, and went to the dinners given by the publisher.

Thackeray's great success as a novelist made him able to build a grand house in Palace Green, 'Millionaires' Row'. Before moving in, he and the girls gave two parties of theatricals in the empty house. The Coles went to the first and thought it 'very well done indeed'.

Thackeray was not to enjoy his grandeur for long, for he died of a long-standing and painful illness, early in the morning of Christmas Eve 1863. Anny and Minny immediately sent for Cole, who searched for the Will, arranged the funeral and helped the girls to arrange their affairs. He got Seymour Haden to dissect the head, to find out the cause of death and save the girls the added grief of an inquest.

When Minny married Leslie Stephen in 1867, Cole gave her a Summerly tea set as a wedding present, and gave her away in church.

21

21 C Wentworth Dilke (1810–1869)

In his family, C Wentworth Dilke was a sort of pig-in-the-middle, caught between his famous father and his unlucky son. All three were named Charles Wentworth. The father was a man of letters, the friend of Keats and Shelley and for many years the editor of *The Athenaeum*. Later he was manager of *The Daily News*, the radical paper for which many of Cole's friends wrote articles. He dominated Cole's friend to the point of almost taking his son away from him and allowing him no say in his education. This son, usually known as Charles Dilke, grew up to be a Liberal politician. He might have been Prime Minister, had he not been cited in a scandalous divorce case. The three generations of Dilkes lived together in London in a house in Sloane Street.

When Cole met them in 1842, he wrote: 'There is a homeliness abt them wh: puts you at your ease'. He and Wentworth Dilke had much in common; in particular they shared a love for and a knowledge of botany. He began to write articles for Dilke's *Gardener's Chronicle*. Then they worked on the *Railway Chronicle*, seeing each other almost every day.

Dilke did not become a member of the Society of Arts until 1849, but as soon as he did he joined

Cole and Scott Russell [22] on the society's Executive Committee for the Great Exhibition. From February 1850, he shared Cole's work under the Royal Commission and had 'Control of the Building and General Superintendence'. After the exhibition closed, he declined a knighthood, wishing for a baronetcy, and he refused all payment for the work he had done. The Queen sent his wife a bracelet with a diamond clasp.

Dilke became one of the inner group that surrounded the Prince, and he advised on how the surplus from the exhibition should be spent. It was while Dilke was staying at Shere [38] that he and Cole had the idea of making the central part of the main quadrangle of the Commissioners' estate into a garden. Dilke had been on the Council of the Royal Horticultural Society for some time, and with Prince Albert as its new president, the negotiations of the lease went smoothly. Dilke laid the Foundation Stone of the new offices for the Society at South Kensington early in 1860.

Dilke was elected chairman of the Society of Arts in 1858 when the idea of holding decennial international exhibitions was brought up. He was enthusiastically in favour of what became the 1862 exhibition, and was one of five trustees that supported it. Afterwards the Queen gave him the baronetcy that he so wanted. He died suddenly at St Petersburg in 1869, where he was an English commissioner at a Russian horticultural exhibition.

22

22   John Scott Russell (1808–1882)

Scott Russell was introduced to Cole by Rowland Hill [11] in August 1844. At that time he was working with Wentworth Dilke [21] on *The Railway Chronicle*, and soon Cole was writing a column each week of 'gossip, the accidents & progress of Works'. To this were soon added Cole's charts and excursions. Russell wrote the technical articles, which he was well qualified to do. Before coming South from Scotland, Russell had made a name for himself as an engineer of great originality. He had designed a successful steam omnibus, and had done research into the behaviour of waves. The Royal Society of Edinburgh had given him their Gold Medal for his paper 'on the laws of resistance of floating bodies'. Several fast steam boats had been built using his discoveries. He was a Vice-President of the Scottish Society of Arts.

In London he was quickly invited to join a committee of the Society of Arts that had been set up to rescue the Society from its financial difficulties. In

the autumn of 1845, he was appointed Secretary and in October he moved into the Secretary house. He had the idea of offering prizes for well-designed household objects, and he and Cole and a few others worked hard to make the exhibitions held by the Society a success. Along with Cole, he was one of the initiators of the Great Exhibition, and together they led committees, made speeches, formed part of deputations. In January 1850, when the Royal Commission was appointed, Russell was made one of the secretaries. He was not a success at this job. Having seen his idea take wing, he was bored by the details. He did not respect the Commissioners and found their long meetings tedious. They disliked his manner and thought him insolent. Lord Granville [27] said that he only bothered to come to meetings on 'state occasions'.

While the work for the exhibition was beginning, Russell's career as a marine engineer was picking up again. In July 1849 Marian Cole launched his ship *The Manchester*. Ships to his design were being built in Prussia and Belgium and he often had to go abroad. In 1849, too, he became a member of the Institution of Civil Engineers, and more prestigiously, he was elected a Fellow of the Royal Society. At the same time, he was paying someone to do his work for him at the Society of Arts and finally resigned the secretaryship in January 1850. Cole, who like everyone from the Prince downwards, was irritated by Russell's inattention to paper work, pressed for him to give up the Society's house with a conspicuous lack of tact.

At the close of the Exhibition, Russell received a hand-written letter from Prince Albert, but no decoration. His rudeness had done it, and his hard work over the six years before was forgotten. He took his place, however, in the group portrait of the Prince's team [29]. He became a director of the company that bought the Crystal Palace, and re-erected it at Sydenham. For many years he lived close to it.

In 1852, Russell began his collaboration with Brunel on the design and building of *The Great Eastern*, 'the finest ship in the world', which was built to steam to Australia without taking on coal. It was a failure and resulted in Russell being threatened with bankruptcy. He had also built several smaller ships during the Crimean War.

He rejoined the Society of Arts, as soon as he ceased being the Secretary, was voted on to the Council and became a Vice-President, Like Cole and Wentworth Dilke he wanted to hold a second Great Exhibition in 1861. Always interested in education, he later sat on a committee including Lord Granville, Lyon Playfair, Dilke and Cole, which tried to hasten the reform of the educational system. He was against 'payment on results'.

Russell could be rude and impatient, and Cole was impressed one day early in their acquaintance, when he saw him knock a man to the ground at Sydenham Station for getting in his way. He was also, however, generous, urbane and possessed a good deal of charm. He and Cole remained friends, in spite of their occasional clashes, when neither was ready to play second fiddle to the other. The Russells often stayed with the Coles at Shere [38], and in 1869, when Alice Russell was married, Cole proposed the health of the bride's parents at the wedding.

23

23 Herbert Minton (1793–1858)

In November 1842 Cole and his wife gave a dinner party at their house in Campden Hill Square. At it were Mr and Mrs C W Dilke and C Wentworth Dilke [21], Mr and Mrs Edwin Chadwick, Thomas Willement and two of Cole's brothers, Lindsay and Richard. After dinner, Horace Grant brought in Herbert Minton, and Charles Cole and three cousins joined them for tea. This was how Cole first met the head of the famous china factory at Stoke-on-Trent. They became friends and later collaborators in Cole's Art-Manufactures. After Minton's death, Matthew Digby Wyatt paid tribute

to him at the Society of Arts:

Of that apparently inexhaustible activity, intellectual and physical, which has formed the dominant characteristic of the past half-century, Mr Minton offered a perfect Type. . . . Neither a man of profound research nor an educated artist, neither an economist nor an inventor, by courage and ceaseless energy he brought to bear upon the creation of his ultimately colossal business, such a combination of science, art, organisation and invention as can be paralleled only by that rare union of qualities which impressed the stamp of genius upon his great predecessor, Josiah Wedgwood.

Cole was less high-flown when he wrote that Minton was 'a very simple good humoured person & fond of fun'. Minton, too, enjoyed Cole's company. After the close of the 1851 Exhibition, they went together to Vienna, to deliver a dessert service made by Mintons that the Queen sent to the Emperor of Austria. On their return Minton wrote to Cole: 'I find your share of Expenses came to £46.19.1. I have therefore entered in my private Cash Book "for the pleasure of Hy Cole's Company for 5 weeks, £46.19.1., rather more than 5Gns pr week, very cheap" '.

A month later he wrote again: 'I am glad to hear that you have taken office in the management of the Schl of Design. You may be *very useful* if you will only be more mild & gentle than you usually are. Not so obstinate & dictatorial, and believe that *you* may sometimes be *wrong & others right*. I hope this plain speaking may not prove unpalatable'.

The two men remained friends and Cole kept the letter among his private papers. In 1855 they were both in Paris for the International Exhibition there, and Minton showed Cole photographs of a collection that belonged to a Madame Soulages at Toulouse. It was an important collection, mainly of Italian pottery, that Cole finally managed to acquire for the South Kensington Museum.

Minton died, aged 65, at his seaside house at Torquay and was succeeded by his two nephews. Cole kept up the connection with them, and the firm supplied mosaics for the museum buildings and for the Albert Hall. The ceramic staircase in the museum was made by them, and the little memorial plaques to Cole's two dogs, Tycho and Jim, can be seen on the wall of the south side of the museum quadrangle.

24 The Felix Summerly Tea service

Cole was in the habit of saying that this tea-set, designed by himself, marked the beginnings of the Great Exhibition. This is true, though it was the friendship between Cole and Scott Russell [22] and their connection with some of the more active members of the Society of Arts that really set things in motion.

In December 1845, Russell and Cole discussed prizes for good design, and the next day Russell offered the Council of the Society £50 towards a fund for prizes. He did so anonymously, 'through the Secretary'. The prizes were to be for 'useful objects calculated to improve the public taste'.

Cole decided to compete, and he managed to persuade Minton to exhibit too. Cole took a great deal of trouble over his design. He went to the British Museum and made drawings of Roman pottery. Then he went to Minton's factory at Stoke-on-Trent, where he spent three days turning the service with the help of the workmen. Everything was

24

carefully worked out: the cup was deep so that it did not cool quickly, and the jug had three lips, in the Etruscan manner, so that it could be poured left- or right-handed. On 23 May 1846, Cole wrote in his diary: 'To Soc of Arts to decide prizes: Sir W Ross, Wyon & c present. Prizes to Mintons 2 Jugs: Medal to Toilette Service & prize to my Tea Service'.

In August Cole got Russell to write to Prince Albert with the result that they were invited to call: the Prince 'admired the Milkpot, but sd the gilding was inferior to the French'. Cole must have shown him the more expensive, gilded version, of the tea set. The service shown at the exhibition had been in red clay and unglazed. The set shown here belongs to the Victoria and Albert Museum and was bought in 1901.

Commercially, the tea service was an enormous success. Hundreds of thousands were made by Mintons and exported all over the world. In 1875, the factory was still making and selling as many as it could produce.

25 A Group of Felix Summerly Art-Manufactures

The 'Bride's Inkstand', one of the first art-manu-factures to be issued in 1847, is on the left. It was designed by John Bell [18]. Several versions were sold, in china, coloured or gilt according to the price, and in silver plate. When made of bronze, Cole called it the 'Bridegroom's Inkstand'. The one shown here is a medium-priced example, as it is coloured, but not gilded. Next is a silver Christening mug, with embossed figures of guardian angels, designed by Richard Redgrave [17]. The 'Well-spring Vase' in the centre, was also designed by him. He designed a clear glass water carafe, with a similar decoration of water weeds. J C Horsley designed the set of decanter stoppers, which illustrate three stages in wine-making. On the right is 'Dorothea' by John Bell, the most successful of all the objects sold.

Most of the Parian figures, like Dorothea, were made by Herbert Minton [23], as was the ink-stand and the vase. For silver items Cole went to Benjamin Smith, a well-known London silversmith. Among other firms employed were Pellatts and I F Christys for glass, Jennens and Bettridge for papier maché, Hollands for furniture and the Coalbrook-dale Iron Company.

The Art-Manufactures were sold through a shop belonging to Cole's friend and publisher, Joseph Cundall in Bond Street, and later about fifteen other shops stocked them as well. Cole's aim was to improve the public's taste by offering household items designed by the best artists and made by the best makers. Though his little enterprise was an innovation and it has taken its place in the history of the decorative arts of the 19th century, for Cole himself it was not a success. Financially it only just broke even, and the news of his involvement in it got around so that in later years his opponents could say that he was a shop-keeper.

25

26 Albert Prince Consort of England (1819–1861)

Prince Albert, a serious, handsome, clever young man, the younger son of the Duke of Saxe-Coburg-Gotha, married the Queen of England on 10 February 1840. In the damp winter dusk of that day Cole and his wife watched the couple drive along Kensington High Street on their way to Windsor Castle for their honeymoon. Cole recorded in his diary that they both looked 'very pleased'.

About eighteen months later the Prince gave away the prizes at the School of Design. Cole was there and wrote of him: 'He seemed a very modest yet sensible man with a mild & tender expression. I was much prepossessed with him'.

Cole was presented to him in February 1842, when he came to inspect the store of public records in the disused riding school of Carlton House. He admired the new cupboards and the colour-coded filing system that Cole had installed, and said afterwards that if he ever wanted to pack the greatest number into the smallest space he would send for Cole.

It was the Society of Arts that brought the Prince and Cole into partnership, if a royal prince and a junior civil servant can ever be called partners. Cole joined early in 1846, and in the years leading up to the Great Exhibition the two men became very close. Cole, who never had any false pride, was ready to do tasks that the courtiers and politicians nearer the Prince could not be asked to perform. He would take dictation, run errands and bring the prince the latest news and gossip. Both men possessed a lofty idealism and a desire to do good, which was linked to a readiness to work hard at details. An unusual combination.

For six months after the appointment of the Royal Commission in January 1850, the Prince went through great frustration at the lack of preparations. In March he thought of giving up. Lord Granville wrote to the prince's secretary, Colonel Grey saying that His Royal Highness 'appears to be almost the only person who has considered the subject both as a whole and in its details. The whole thing would fall to pieces, if he left it to itself'. The Prince was terribly overworked. The Queen, who had no private secretary, was expecting their seventh child, and the Prince was dealing with her official papers and bearing the brunt of the difficulties with the Foreign Secretary, Lord Palmerston. To this was added the worries about the exhibition; about the lack of a building, about opposition to holding it in Hyde Park, about the lack of money. On the 2nd July the Prince wrote to his old friend from Coburg, Baron Stockmar: 'We are on the point of having to abandon the exhibition altogether'. Under the strain he had

26

become exhausted, slept badly and woke early and had stomach pains. The Queen also wrote to Baron Stockmar that he was being 'shamefully plagued about the Exhibition'.

The opposition to the site reached a climax on 4 July in a debate and division in the House of Commons. In the morning, Cole called on several Members of Parliament to give them a paper he had written in favour of Hyde Park. In the evening he listened to the debate and after the division took the good news of the result to Buckingham Palace. The Prince called him up to his private room, where Cole found him 'very nervous'. The Prince said he would have given up the exhibition, rather than hold it anywhere else, and added that it was 'like asking your friends to your flower garden and putting them among the cabbages'.

About ten days later, Cole got a businessman to launch the guarantee fund with £35,000. Then he called on Colonel Grey with the news. The Prince came in and sat on the edge of the table to hear the details, and said: 'Now is the time for work. It is not plans that are wanted'.

When the exhibition was over Prince Albert wrote Cole a letter in his own hand. Part of it ran:

'You have been one of the few who originated the design, became its exponent to the public, and fought its battles in adversity, and belong now to those who share its triumphs, and it must be as pleasing to you to reflect how much you have contributed to them by your untiring exertions, as it is to me to acknowledge my sense of them'.

The Queen could write of the exhibits: '. . . our people have shown such taste in their manufacturers!' But to most people it was evident that British design was inferior to that of other countries. The Prince gave Cole his support in his work to reform the Schools of Design. They never forgot that their ultimate aim was to increase trade by improving British goods. The Prince's interest was not mere patronage; he took a real and personal interest in Cole's projects, particularly in the museum. When the time came for the move to South Kensington, he went there himself, chose the exact position for the 'boilers' and paced out the foundations. He remained interested in the later buildings, and directed the planning of the rest of the Commissioners' estate. Gradually he became ill more and more often, and when the 1861 (later 1862) exhibition was mooted, he had no energy left to face the difficulties and work all over again. He died of typhoid fever on 14 December 1861. A week later Lord Granville saw the Queen and when Cole was mentioned, she said: 'No-one would be more sensible of his loss'.

27 Earl Granville (1815–1891)

In the summer of 1848 the headmaster of the School of Design resigned, and it looked as though the school would have to close. Charles Buller [7] suggested to Lord Granville, who was Vice-President of the Board of Trade, that Cole might be able to give helpful advice. Lord Granville, who, like everyone, knew Cole's reputation as a troublemaker, asked warily, 'Will he get me into a scrape?' Buller answered that he had never done so with him. So Cole was asked to call. Lord Granville thought him 'most disagreeable', and told him so many years later after they had become friends. However, within a few days of their first meeting, he asked him to dinner, where he met Lords Radnor, Minto, Bessborough, Morpeth and Clanricarde, and Sir E Bulwer.

Over the next few months Cole wrote three reports for Lord Granville, giving his ideas of how the Government should make use of the Schools of Design for the decoration of official buildings; how designs should be copyrighted; how the School itself should be organised. At the same time he brought

out a magazine, *The Journal of Design*, to campaign for changes at the schools and an improvement in public taste generally. Small pieces of real cloth or wallpaper were tipped in to demonstrate what was good taste. Cole persevered with it until he joined the Board of Trade, though Charles Cole, one of his brothers, took over the editorship when Cole became preoccupied with the 1851 Exhibition.

Granville George Leveson-Gower, second Earl Granville, usually known as Pussy, was the best-connected young Whig politician of the day and one of the richest. The Duke of Devonshire was his uncle; the Duke of Sutherland was his cousin. Charles Greville, the diarist (and a grandson of the Duke of Portland) was also a cousin and shared his house in London. Whether the Whigs were in power or not, Lord Granville had influence and patronage to assist Cole. In his political career he became Lord President of the Council, Secretary for the Colonies, twice Foreign Secretary, Leader of the House of Lords and twice almost Prime Minister.

This photograph of Lord and Lady Granville (she was the daughter of the Duc de Dalberg) comes from the Cole family album and dates from about 1856. It was in that year that Lord Granville headed a special mission to Russia to represent the Queen at the coronation of the Czar Nicholas II. He took with him a large suite of attachés, secretaries, servants and Corporal Spackman, a Sapper photographer lent by Cole from South Kensington. He

27

also bought some vases from Herbert Minton which were, as he wrote, 'scattered about' his house in Moscow, 'and added very much to the effect'.

Richard Redgrave once stayed with a mill-owner at Manchester when Lord Granville was also there, and wrote in his diary that: 'Lord Granville has much *bonhomie*, and there is strong common sense in his views of things. He was very pleasant and agreeable, and the contrast between rank and manufacture was a study. Lord Granville is full of anecdote – an incessant story-telling. He kept us alive with story after story . . . till past one'.

At the opening of the International Exhibition of 1862, onlookers were amused to see Lord Granville 'broom in hand, vigourously sweeping the carpet in front of the state chairs only a few moments before he had to rush off to receive the Duke of Cambridge'. Lord Granville had no need to stand on dignity.

28 Dr Lyon Playfair (1818–1892)

Cole's colleague during the preparations for the Great Exhibition, Playfair was by training a scientist. He had been the favourite student of the great German chemist, Baron von Liebig and had translated his book on agricultural chemistry into English. Through his scientific friends he had met Sir Robert Peel, who arranged for him to advise Prince Albert on an invention of his for the disposal of sewage. Playfair became a scientific committee man, sitting regularly on Royal Commissions. Playfair was even shorter than Cole and like him wore spectacles. When Cole first met him he was thirty-two and already a bit plump. He had a twinkling sense of humour and Cole enjoyed his indecent stories. He was said to be 'one of those men of exceptional personal and social gifts, before whose tact difficulties . . . melt away, and whose bright spirits create around them an atmosphere of good-will and confidence which is recognised by all with whom they are destined to be brought into contact'. This tact was well tested when the Great Exhibition was being planned.

When things were going so badly in June 1850, Sir Robert Peel and Lord Granville, both of them Cabinet Ministers and therefore Royal Commissioners, arranged for Playfair to be appointed an Assistant Commissioner to sit in on the Commission's meetings and report to the Executive Committee. Within two days of his appointment, Playfair happened to meet Cole in Whitehall and Cole burst out that the exhibition was doomed to failure and that he was going to resign and had his letter of resignation in his pocket. Playfair described how he

took him by the arm and walked him gently up and down the street and 'urged that as he was the real pilot of the vessel, it was a wrong act to desert the sinking ship'. He told Cole that manufacturers could be 'aroused to the importance of the undertaking' and Cole at last agreed to destroy his letter and carry on. 'Had the accidental meeting not taken place, the Great Exhibition would never have been held, for its mainspring would have been broken'.

In his autobiography Playfair says this of Cole:

He was a man of remarkable energy and ability, and had no other object in regard to any work in which he was engaged than the best method of ensuring its success. He has often been accused of working from selfish motives. Never was an accusation more unfounded. The public good was always the uppermost – I might say the only – motive in his mind. He was constantly misjudged, because his modes of work were not always on the surface. If he came to an obstacle, it was his delight to tunnel under it in secret, and unexpectedly come out at the other side. His purposes were, therefore, not unfrequently misunderstood, and when I joined the Executive there was much want of confidence between it and the Royal Commission. This was unjust to Cole, with whom I was constantly associated to the end of his life, and for whom I had a sincere respect.

At the close of the Exhibition both men were made Companions of the Bath, and Playfair was invited to become a Gentleman Usher in Prince Albert's household.

They continued to work together in the Department of Practical Art, and the Science and Art Department. In 1858 Playfair went home to Edinburgh to be Professor of Chemistry, but they still met often in London. Playfair was particularly good at managing the juries of the various international exhibitions, and at giving dinners for jurors and exhibitors.

Later he became a Member of Parliament and was Speaker of the House of Commons in the 1880s. In 1892 he was created Baron Playfair of St Andrews.

29 Prince Albert and the Organisers of the Great Exhibition

This painting is always known as 'The Royal Commissioners for the Exhibition of 1851', although eighteen Commissioners are not shown and four portraits are of men who, like Cole, were not Commissioners at all.

Prince Albert [26] holds some drawings for the Crystal Palace, with a model of the Duke of Devonshire's Great Conservatory at his elbow. The Duke's gardener, Joseph Paxton, who designed that greenhouse and the Crystal Palace, leans on the table to the Prince's right. William Cubitt sits holding a pair

of dividers and Lord Stanley (later the 14th Earl of Derby) sits opposite. Standing on the left of the picture are the two most active members of the Executive Committee, C Wentworth Dilke [21] and Cole, with John Scott Russell [22] between them. In front sit Richard Cobden, Charles Barry and Lord Granville [27]. The other standing figures are, left to right, Charles Fox, who was a partner in the firm that built the Crystal Palace, Paxton, Lord John Russell, Sir Robert Peel and Robert Stephenson.

30 The Opening Ceremony of the Great Exhibition

The 1st of May 1851. The great day had arrived! The moment in the ceremony recorded here is when the Archbishop of Canterbury said a 'short and appropriate prayer', which was followed by the Hallelujah Chorus sung by massed choirs. During the music, the Chinese gentleman came forward and made a low bow to the Queen. He was not there in any official capacity, but Colonel Owen had the presence of mind to place him in the procession of Commissioners and foreign representatives that toured the building, before the Lord Chamberlain was commanded by the Queen to declare the Exhibition open.

Cole is one of the group on the left. The tall figure at the edge of the painting is Colonel Lloyd and

29

30

next to him, and gazing out of the picture, is Lyon Playfair. They worked together as liaison officers between the Commission and local committees. In front of Playfair is Joseph Paxton with his hat under his arm, and next to him is Charles Fox, whose firm built the Crystal Palace. The bearded face peering over his shoulder belongs to Owen Jones, who designed the colour scheme of the building. Next stands Cole, well forward and almost obscuring the Chairman of the Executive Committee, Colonel Reid. His face, in turn, almost hides Wentworth Dilke's. Away to the right, next to the column under the gallery, and showing a large, white shirt-front, is Warren de la Rue, a member of the family of famous printers and paper-makers. With one of Rowland Hill's brothers he had invented an envelope-making machine, and later he became an astro-physicist. He was a member of the Society of Arts and was a friend of Cole's. He commissioned this painting and it was given to the South Kensington Museum after his death in 1889.

The painting was begun within a few weeks of the opening of the Exhibition, and there was some undignified manoeuvring to get the best places. Cole's portrait was painted twice, but his diary does not make it clear whether he, or the painter, was dissatisfied with the first attempt.

31 The Valentine 1852

Thackeray habitually made little drawings in the letters and notes that he sent people. This is one he sent Cole. He sent one to Alan Cole at the same time. As is often the case with jokes, there is an undercurrent of truth in Thackeray's little verse. Many of Cole's friends thought that he would get a knighthood for his work for the Great Exhibition, and were disappointed when he was made a Companion of the Bath, the standard decoration for a long-serving civil servant. The sketch shows Cole as his contemporaries were used to see him, wearing a pair of spectacles.

32 A Gallery in the Museum of Ornamental Art

Cole's first museum was in five rooms at Marlborough House and opened in May 1852. All the rooms, like this one, were domestic in scale, and were quickly filled with a mixture of objects bought from the Great Exhibition and loans from the Royal Collection and several rich collectors. Soon new purchases began to be added to the display. In one gallery Cole set out a collection of objects, which he and his colleagues thought were designed on 'False Principles', to demonstrate to the public what was bad taste. It appealed to Dickens's sense of humour,

The Quean I sea
That Rawyal Sole
'Rise hup (seshee)
Sir Ennary Cole!'
And now at Vin
-ser Castle dine;
And be my Ansum
Walentine.

31

and he published a piece about it in *Household Words*. In a story called 'House full of Horrors' the mortification of Mr Crumpet of Crump Lodge, Brixton, was described after he found that almost all the furnishings of his comfortable house were hung up in the museum as examples of bad design. The manufacturers of the 'horrors' were indignant that a department of the Board of Trade should give them such adverse publicity, and they complained so loudly, that within six months the display had to be taken down. Charles Robinson, who was in charge of the museum was delighted when it went. It is a disappointment that so little is known about this gallery, though a few of the objects have been traced in the museum's collections. The painter of this water-colour, William Casey, who recorded several of the rooms, was an Irishman who had been a student at Marlborough House. He was the Headmaster of the St Martin's School, and painted this picture not long before the museum was dismantled for the move to South Kensington.

33 The Duke of Wellington Funeral Car (*overleaf*)

The funeral of the Duke of Wellington on 18 November 1852, was the greatest public spectacle of the nineteenth Century. The hearse, or 'funeral car', is seen in this print at Hyde Park Corner, opposite the Duke's London House, on its way from Whitehall to St Paul's Cathedral. The day was proclaimed a bank holiday and one-and-a-half million people watched the two-and-a-half-hour procession of soldiers and mourning carriages.

The Duke died at Walmer Castle on 14 September and the Queen ordered the body to be taken over by the Crown so that a state funeral could be arranged. The body waited at Walmer Castle sealed up inside four coffins of pine, lead, oak and polished Spanish mahogany.

The design of the funeral car was at first left to the Royal undertaker, William Banting, who became famous ten years later when he went on a high-protein diet, lost forty-six pounds and gave his name to slimming. The designs he showed to Prince Albert were typical upholsterers' confections of elaborate hangings over a wooden frame. The Prince did not think them good enough for the hero of Waterloo and on 21 October the Lord Chamberlain went to see Cole and Redgrave at Marlborough House.

It was the first time that the Schools of Design had received a public commission and Cole grasped the chance with both hands. He went out straight away to measure the arch of Temple Bar and then he and Redgrave had a discussion and decided that the carriage should be of bronze: 'a real substantial work . . . thoroughly simple, as was the character of the Duke, the only decorations being the pall, the armorial bearings . . . and the names of his great battles'. Redgrave made a sketch design and when they showed it to the Prince two days later he exclaimed, 'This is the thing!'

Other members of the staff at Marlborough House designed the details, students did the working drawings and the female art students did much of the embroidery. Cole and Redgrave worked day and night seeing Banting and court officials and superin-

41

42

33

tending the work as it went along. The car, 27 feet long, 10 feet wide and 17 feet high, was finished in three weeks, when it would normally have taken a full year. The bronze castings were made by several firms in London, Birmingham and Sheffield, and were assembled inside an 'immense ordnance tent' on Horseguards Parade. On the day before the funeral Cole noticed that the workmen were 'nearly worn out with fatigue'.

The day of the funeral was an anxious one for Cole, Redgrave and their colleagues. They were relieved when the car finally rolled out of the tent, drawn by twelve black horses lent by Booth's gin distillery and they followed the procession some way along the route, but were both too tired to go to St Paul's Cathedral.

A friend of Lord Granville's watched from a house in Piccadilly and wrote in his *Recollections* that 'it was a moving sight which even the horrible South Kensington catafalque with all its tawdry vulgarities, could not altogether deprive of its solemnity'.

34

34 Sir (John) Charles Robinson (1824–1913)

Charles Robinson was the first keeper of the Museum of Ornamental Art, and it was he who founded the museum's superb collection of Italian Renaissance sculpture.

He was a born collector. When he was twenty he was sent to Paris to study painting, but spent most of his time at the Louvre or in antique shops. He made tours of the countryside and was deeply moved by Gothic art and architecture. In 1851 he visited Italy, and from Florence he sent a letter to his close friend William Maw-Egley, the painter of this miniature. It was a hot night in July and he had 'a famous stout flask of Montepulciano' beside him as he wrote: 'I have just got in from a long ramble thro' the town after dark, . . . quite in a state of beatitude. . . . Consider here I am, within a stones throw of the finest things the world has ever seen in art; before me is Michael Angelos David!–I lean against the Pedestal of Benvenuto Cellini's Perseus;–here is Donatellos Judith, there is John of Bolognas grand works;–close by Ghiberti's Gates–the gates of Paradise . . . I cannot enumerate them.–all are around.–I have been cold and unmoved till now; but if ever man has had communion with the spirits of the departed I have done so this night; . . . the people here I fancy think I am half mad'.

When Robinson wrote this he was 27 years old and was the headmaster of a Government School of Design near Stoke-on-Trent, where he had become friendly with Herbert Minton. Perhaps because of this friendship and a recommendation to Cole he was appointed in 1852 a Teachers Training Master at the London School of Design. Soon though, his other talents showed themselves and he was given the post of superintendent of the museum at Marlborough House.

Robinson and Cole worked together smoothly for some years, but after the move to South Kensington, Robinson asked to be given the title of Director, rather than Keeper. This was not allowed. Then he refused to keep an official diary of how he spent his time in the office. He ignored modern works of art and bought more and more Renaissance sculpture, so that the museum was nick-named 'a post classical British Museum'. In 1863, the Board issued a sharp minute to remind him of the department's policy of making purchases that were 'applicable to utility'. Robinson resigned his keepership, but continued to act as a consultant, or 'Art Referee'. In this capacity he became increasingly authoritarian. He resented having to submit the works he chose as purchases to the board. He disliked being told to consult with other experts. He wanted the title of Art Referee aggrandised. He wrote letters direct to the Board, instead of through the proper channel–that is, Cole, who was the secretary. The row reverberated round the Department, with the staff siding with Cole. One has sympathy for

35

in advising other collectors. When Redgrave resigned the surveyorship of the Queen's pictures, Sir Philip Cunliffe-Owen [35] suggested that Robinson should succeed him, which caused jealousy at the Royal Academy, as up to that time, the Surveyor had always been an Academician.

Robinson was knighted in 1887, and developed into a courtly old gentleman with a long white beard. He bought a manor house near Swanage in Dorset, where he entertained his grand-children amongst his collection of armour, sculpture and Chinese porcelain. It is sad to learn that many of his medieval objects were discovered to be fakes, and were the centre of acrimonious discussions at the Society of Antiquaries.

35 Sir (Francis) Philip Cunliffe-Owen (1828–1894)

Cunliffe-Owen succeeded Cole as Director of the South Kensington Museum on Cole's retirement in 1873. He was the younger brother of Colonel Henry Owen, R E who became a friend of Cole's during the preparations for the Great Exhibition, and who worked closely with him until the beginning of the Crimean War. Their father was a Captain in the Royal Navy and Philip joined the navy when he was twelve; but after five years he was invalided out. Through his brother he joined the team working on the British section of the Paris Exhibition of 1855, and remained with Cole in his department, rising to be Assistant Director of the Museum by 1860.

After his death, *The Times* wrote of him: 'he was neither more or less than a capable man of business; he had little expert knowledge, and perhaps hardly valued it enough in those who possessed it'. He recognised this himself, and told Cole that his work was to carry out what Cole had originated, and that he was only an administrator.

What Owen really enjoyed was organising exhibitions and putting on displays. After his initiation in Paris in 1855, he worked in London, Vienna, Philadelphia and Paris again. In 1883 he arranged a Fisheries Exhibition at South Kensington, into which he 'introduced an element of amusement and popularity, and the Fisheries exhibition became the fashionable lounge of London for the summer'.

He thoroughly enjoyed the popularity that his hard work brought him, particularly when in 1878 the Prince of Wales recommended him for a KCMG. As the *Times* obituarist waspishly put it: 'His taste for orders was gratified also by a large number of foreign decorations'.

Robinson. Time after time in Italy or Spain he found marvellous works of art that could be bought for ridiculously low sums of money, but his inspired buying was controlled from London by Cole, Redgrave and their Lordships.

The storm broke in the autumn of 1867 when it was discovered that while travelling at the Department's expense, Robinson was dealing for himself and for his private clients. In January 1868, his post was abolished, and he was given six months' notice. He wrote furious letters to their Lordships and rushed to see Gladstone and Lord Granville [27]. Lord Granville told him that he could not interfere with the working of the office, and pointed out that he, Robinson, was not 'very amenable to official rules and discipline'. Lord Granville also wrote to Cole: 'I suspect it is a mistake of yours to lose his services, and to get into a row with all his dilettante friends'.

The true reason for the dismissal was hushed up. Thirty years later Donnelly wrote to Lyon Playfair saying: 'I ought to have pressed at the time to have the case made known. But I did not want to ruin the man: and poor Owen was in a foolish way sadly mixed up in it. The consequence has been that I have been persecuted by the fellow ever since'.

Robinson was still occasionally consulted by the museum, but his fame lay in his own collecting and

36 Captain Francis Fowke RE (1823–1865)

Fowke (pronounced 'folk') first became known to Cole through Colonel Owen, who brought him into the team for the Paris Exhibition of 1855. Fowke became Secretary of the British Commission when Owen returned to real soldiering and went to the Crimean War. In 1856, Fowke was appointed Inspector for Science and Art and was put in charge of doing up 'the nest of old buildings' at South Kensington. He already had experience of architectural work in the army, as he had designed and built some barracks at Devonport.

He arrived in the department with a reputation as an inventor. He had designed a drawbridge and some floating pontoons. He had realised before Whitworth that an elongated bullet would be more accurate than a ball when fired from a rifle. While he was working for the department Cole said that he developed, among other things, 'a very portable military fire-engine, which has been adopted in the army; a collapsing camera; an improved umbrella . . . a portable bath to pack up like a book; also a lighting machine which is used throughout the Kensington Museum, and by means of which hundreds of gas burners are lighted in a few seconds'. Fowke was also a good horseman and an accomplished figure-skater.

Fowke designed the first permanent building at South Kensington, the gallery to house the collection of pictures given by John Sheepshanks. Soon he had an office of assistants, and, in consultation with Cole and Redgrave, designed galleries and offices for the museum, the buildings for the International Exhibition of 1862, and the Great Conservatory for the Royal Horticultural Society's Gardens [43]. He designed the Royal Scottish Museum in Edinburgh and added to the National Gallery in Dublin. The Prince Consort gave him a private commission to design a library for the officers at Aldershot.

Professional architects were much displeased that mere soldiers were doing so much design work on the Commissioners' Estate, and neither Fowke, nor his successor, Henry Scott [37] were elected members of the Royal Institution of British Architects. In 1864 a row broke out when a competition was held for designs for the Natural History Museum, which was to go where the 1862 buildings had stood. The designs were, of course, submitted anonymously to a panel consisting mainly of professional architects, and it was Fowke's that won. After Fowke's death, Alfred Waterhouse took over the project, and Fowke's design was abandoned.

One of Fowke's colleagues, Capt Donnelly RE, said that he had a mind, which 'though essentially practical, was wonderfully pliant and original'.

Dilke who at the time was fed up with the delays in completing the Horticultural Gardens, told Cole that he was 'as clever as possible – but no man of business'. Cole himself wrote some six months after Fowke's death that 'constitutionally, nature had given Captain Fowke a sluggish and indolent temperament, but he was roused to prompt action occasionally'.

Poor Fowke was unhappily married, which may be why he sometimes lacked energy. His wife was a stout lady, with dark hair and a tight little mouth between protruding cheeks. She so disliked their son, another Francis, known as Frank, that for years he lived with his grandmother. Frank remembered his father's 'coldness' and his mother's untidiness, extravagance and attacks of hysterics. Sometimes the two did not speak for days.

In 1865, Fowke overworked himself designing and superintending the buildings for the museum, and making drawings and a model for the Royal Albert Hall [47]. He went to Switzerland and to Eastbourne, but died at the beginning of December of that year. Five years later Frank Fowke married Cole's fourth daughter, Isabella.

37

37 Major-General Henry Y D Scott RE (1822–1883)

Like Fowke Scott was a Royal Engineer who was brought into the Cole circle for his managerial capabilities. He came to South Kensington, with the rank of Major, in 1864 to help Cole run the Horticultural Gardens. Cole, Redgrave and Fowke had known of him for at least seven years before that, because a cement invented by him was used for all the new buildings at South Kensington from the time in was patented in 1857. At that time Scott was a Senior Instructor at Woolwich. Later, he was at Chatham where he made experiments with selenitic lime and the composition of mortar.

On the very day that Fowke died in December 1865, Cole asked Scott if he would like to succeed him, and so he superintended the building and decorating of the Royal Albert Hall [47], according to the model made by Fowke and Sergeant Spackman. He was appointed Director for New Buildings at the museum, where he continued to use Fowke's red brick and terra cotta and, again like Fowke, he was closely supervised by Cole and Redgrave. Scott was not resentful, and got on well with Cole, acknowledging that he 'gave up everything for art'.

Scott and his family often stayed with the Coles at Shere [38] and the two men so enjoyed talking 'shop', that to prevent it when they were supposed to be on holiday, they fined themselves 1/–.

Scott's wife, Selena, was the daughter of a Major-General and they had fifteen living children, so Scott was constantly looking for ways to augment his official salary of £750 a year. They lived economically at Ealing and nearby Scott had an experimental works that turned sewage into manure. Some of the dry matter was baked in kilns and made into cement. Outside his official work, Scott was Secretary of the 1851 Commissioners from 1869 to 1882, which was paid, and he was honorary secretary of the Royal Horticultural Society from 1866 to 1873. In 1871 Scott retired from the army as an honorary Major-General, keeping his post at South Kensington. He set up Scott's Sewage Company, with offices in rooms at the Albert Hall. The Chairman was the Duke of Sutherland and the Company Secretary was Redgrave's son Gilbert.

After Cole retired in 1873, he and Scott were not on good terms. Cole lived in a house across the road from the museum, and took to calling on Scott in his office to give him unwanted advice. Cunliffe-Owen tried to suggest to him that he ought not to do it, but Cole took no notice and there were rows. However, their disagreements did not prevent Cole from becoming the Managing Director of the sewage company. It was a failure and had to be wound up in 1879.

In 1882, the Treasury abolished Scott's post at only a few weeks' notice. It was said that money worries hastened his death in the following year.

38 The Cottage at Shere (overleaf)

(a) In 1856
(b) In about 1860
Cole rented Elm Cottage, Shere, in February 1856, when he took the first of these two photographs. The light was very poor and he went over the print in ink. A year later he turned what was a simple workman's cottage, dating from the seventeenth century, into a Victorian *cottage orné*. He added the porch, and the picturesque dormer windows, with Minton tile roundels set in the gables.

Here, in the Surrey hills, halfway between Guildford and Dorking, the Cole children spent most of their summers, Cole going up to London daily by train. Friends and relations visited them and they went for long walks and picnics. Cole joined in village life, helping with the flower show, running concerts and establishing a reading room for the villagers.

The cottage still stands, unchanged, but for a shop built in the garden on one side.

39 Francis Seymour Haden (1818–1910)

This self portrait is the only etching done by Haden in 1862, when so much of his time was taken up by his work as a juror at the London International Exhibition. He was a surgeon by profession, but he is better known as an etcher and art-historian. His contemporaries compared him to Rembrandt: indeed he was one of the first scholars to study Rembrandt's work properly, and to distinguish between the work of the master and that of his followers or imitators.

Haden and Charles Cole (H C's third brother) were friends from schooldays at Christ's Hospital, and Haden was doctor to the whole Cole family, and Cole had him appointed honorary surgeon to the Department of Science and Art. He was married to James McNeill Whistler's half-sister, Deborah (Dasha), and Whistler lived with them when he was a little boy, and Cole's children first met Whistler at a party given by the Dilkes. Alan Cole and Whistler remained friends for life. Haden and Dasha used to stay with the Cole family at Shere, [38], as did Haden's junior partner, James Traer, with

his wife and baby. One of Haden's most-admired etchings is of the mill pond at Shere. Cole etched too, and they bit their plates together in Haden's etching room at the top of his house in Sloane Street; his French printer pulling the proofs.

When Cole decided to build himself a larger country house, he and Haden bought adjacent plots at Witley, a few miles to the West of Shere. Haden did nothing with his land, which exasperated Cole. Harry Cole designed a grand house for his father, with stables and a landscaped garden. Cole had to sell it as soon as it was finished to pay for it.

The friendship between the two men came to an abrupt end in the summer of 1867. Cole arranged for Traer to be appointed a juror at the Paris International Exhibition and Haden objected, saying that as he had to be in Paris himself, Traer could not be spared from the practice. His true reason for objecting was that he knew Traer had become a drunkard, which he told Cole about in confidence. But Haden was known to be irascible and so Cole and his colleagues took no notice, believing that Haden was being unjust. Even when Traer died in Paris, and Haden showed them a

doctor's certificate giving the cause of death as *delirium tremens*, some still thought that it was only an epileptic fit. Whistler, who was a great friend of Traer's was so infuriated that he punched Haden in the street. Back in London, Haden resigned his post in the Science and Art Department, and published a pamphlet about the affair.

Like so many men in the 19th century, Haden was interested in sanitary reform. While people like Chadwick and Cole were interested in drains and sewers, he turned his attention to the burial of the dead. With the enormous expansion of towns in the first half of the 19th century, the graveyards that surrounded the parish churches had become disgustingly full, and by about the middle of the century, it was realised that the smell might be associated with disease. According to Seymour Haden, the trouble was made worse by the habit of burying bodies in airtight, thick wooden coffins, which were almost indestructible. He maintained that if coffins made of *papier mâché* or wicker were used, then the earth could do its work, and the grave could be re-used in about six years. A late-20th century gardener would call the process 'composting'. In 1875, he published two pamphlets, and founded the 'Earth to Earth Society'. In the

middle of the Summer, when the social season was at its height, the Duke of Sutherland [50] allowed him to hold a private view of his coffins on the terrace of Stafford House. It was reported in a weekly paper that Rotten Row and other resorts were emptied, and the whole fashionable world crowded to see the twelve coffins on display. They were made of osiers, and had 'the appearance of extra-sized bassinets for very large babies'. Some were painted white, or stained in stripes of blue, or black and gold. A few were lined with moss, which 'a lady remarked "looked snugger" ' than the unlined ones, which suggested 'cool summer wear'.

40   The Grounds of the South Kensington Museum in 1862

This romantic moonlit view of the Western side of the museum's grounds shows Brompton Park House with the East dome of the 1862 International Exhibition building glimmering from the other side of Exhibition Road. The house was lived in by the museum's Deputy Superintendant, Philip Cunliffe-Owen [35]. The far end of the building was used as

41

barracks for the museum's detachment of Sappers. The house was demolished in 1899 to make way for the present front of the museum and the galleries behind it. The two people on the lawn are standing where Room 48 now is.

It looks as though the Cunliffe-Owens are having a party.

41 Robert Lowe (1811–1892)

As can be seen from this portrait of 1875 by his friend George Watts, Lowe was a very handsome man. His white hair is not due to age, but to his being an albino. He had very poor sight, and was told many times by eye specialists that he was certain to go quite blind. Having no coloured pigment to protect his eyes from the light, he found that: 'the eyelids must always be nearly closed and so I have never been able to enjoy the luxury of staring anyone full in the face. . . . I cannot even conceive the state of a person to whom sight is a function free from all pain and distress'. This he wrote in a scrap of autobiography that he began on a typewriter in 1876.

He somehow overcame his difficulties and gained a first class degree in classics at Oxford. He would have had a double first with mathematics if he had not rubbed out part of his paper with his nose.

In 1842, his sight became so bad that he was told that unless he went out to one of the colonies and led an out-of-doors life he would go blind. So he went to Sydney, where to shield his eyes from the glare of the almost sub-tropical sun he had a pair of goggles made out of two spoons with a tiny hole pierced in each bowl. He and his wife built a delightful shady bungalow, Bronte House, that overlooks Nelson Bay (the next bay to Bondi Beach), a few miles from Sydney, and Lowe began a career as a barrister and politician. He played a part in founding the colony of Victoria.

In 1851, he came back to London, was elected to Parliament as a Radical in the following year and immediately impressed the House with his beautiful voice and skill in debate. He was soon given office, and from 1859 to 1864 he was at the Board of Trade and in charge of education under Lord Granville [27]. He was Cole's partner in his battles with Treasury officials, and was delighted when he finally defeated them in the long wrangle over the Soulages collection and enabled Cole to buy it for his museum. He encouraged Cole's building programme at South Kensington, and in 1860 got an extra £10,000 out of the Government for him.

Lowe introduced the system, already existing in primary education, of linking the amount of the government grants to successes in examinations. This 'payments on results' had the effect, in art schools, of turning drawing into examinable exercises. It suited Cole—he was always looking for ways of making rules and laying down 'principles' by which 'good art' might be achieved. He and Redgrave followed their chief's instructions with enthusiasm and the system lasted until 1902. Cole liked and admired Lowe, and in his diary never mentions his blindness, only speaking of his geniality and wit.

Things were quite different after 1868 when Lowe became Chancellor of the Exchequer. He was now on the side of the Treasury and he brought the building programme at the museum to a halt. He tried, too, to turn the museum into a branch of the British Museum, which had a board of fifty trustees, exactly the sort of committee that Cole most abhorred. As if this was not enough, Lowe was an 1851 Commissioner, and opposed the building of the Royal Albert Hall [47], questioning Cole's optimistic estimates of the costs of construction and wanting the Commission to build a much smaller hall of its own.

Lowe left the Treasury at about the same time that Cole retired, and a few months later Cole let his fury burst out at the ceremony to open the new

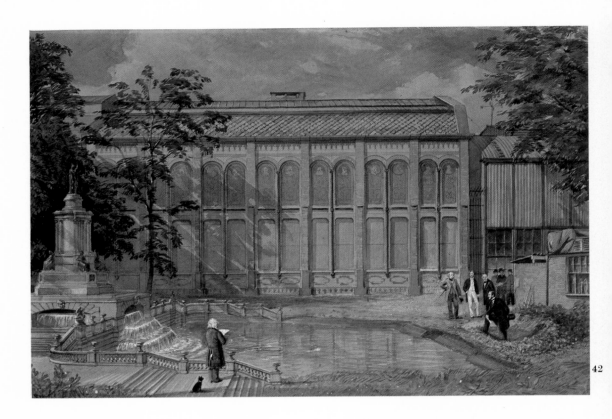

art school at Spitalfields in East London. He said Lowe had 'a flinty bosom', was a 'wilful man', 'a man of very bad judgment', 'no statesman whatever', and nothing but a 'milk and water Rabelais'. No newspapers reported this extraordinary speech though one weekly, *The Spectator*, did, and gave Cole a warning: 'He will find, we suspect, before long the truth of the great axiom in politics that temper never pays.' It was true. His behaviour gave people the excuse not to subscribe to the testimonial fund that his friends collected for him. Mr Lowe was created Lord Sherbrooke in 1880.

42 The Memorial to the Great Exhibition

This water colour shows the quadrangle of the museum in May 1861. A half-scale model of the memorial, designed by Joseph Durham, has been set up beside the museum's ornamental fire tank. The Prince Consort is standing in a trench in order to view it from the best angle. With him are Colonel Grey [46], Francis Fowke [36] and Sydney Smirke, the elderly architect of the Royal Horticultural Society's Gardens [43 & 44]. Henry Cole and Tycho are in the foreground. Behind is the special gallery put up to hold the John Sheepshanks collection of pictures. To the right can be seen the end of the Iron Museum, or 'Boilers'.

The memorial was paid for by public subscription and at first the committee wanted to have a statue of the Prince. He was embarrassed by the idea of a statue being put up during his lifetime, so 'Britannia presiding over the four corners of the Globe' was substituted. Shortly after this painting was done Britannia was changed for a statue of the Queen. John Bell meanwhile campaigned for an obelisk.

When the Prince died in December 1861, the Queen asked for the original idea for a statue of the Prince to be revived, and the Prince of Wales [45] paid for it. After the authorities refused to allow the monument to be put up in Hyde Park, it was made the centrepiece of the Royal Horticultural Society's Gardens.

43

43 The opening of the Royal Horticultural Society's Gardens (*previous page*)

On 5 June 1861 the Prince Consort performed his last public duty when he opened the new gardens in the centre of the Commissioners' Estate, South Kensington. This water colour is of the royal party during the ceremony. (The Queen is not present because of the recent death of her mother, the Duchess of Kent.) It shows inside of the Great Conservatory, designed by Francis Fowke [36].

The gardens, which covered twenty acres between Exhibition Road and Queens Gate, were the result of an uneasy partnership between the Royal Horticultural Society and the Royal Commissioners. The Prince was President of both bodies, and he worried a great deal over the gardens' layout and construction, nearly as much as he had done about the Great Exhibition. The Queen thought that his anxiety over the gardens contributed to his death six months later. Despite this, she felt it to be her 'duty to visit and watch over' the museum, and South Kensington as a whole. She understood Cole, and often calls him 'Good Mr Cole', in her journal, and refers to 'his rough off hand manner'.

To commemorate the Prince's birthday in August 1864, Cole arranged for the gardens to be open free to the public. The Queen heard from General Grey that the 'Fete', as she called it 'had succeeded most admirably & that there were nearly 200,000 persons there & not one flower picked, or bed trodden upon! How gratifying & how it speaks of the respect & love for my dearest one!'

Afterwards she sent Cole a small bronze bust of the Prince.

44 The Royal Horticultural Society's Gardens from the North

This view of the gardens is taken from the roof of the great conservatory, looking South-east. The memorial to the Great Exhibition [42] is in the middle of the picture, and behind are the buildings of the 1862 exhibition. To the left a ray of sunshine lights up the South Kensington Museum.

The water colour must have been done between the unveiling of the memorial in June 1863 and the demolition of the exhibition buildings in the Autumn of 1864 (Lieut. Knocker R E was in charge of blowing up the main arches). This was when the gardens were at their most fashionable. They were semi-private and only open to Fellows of the Royal Horticultural Society and certain other paying customers. Cole joined the Council of the Society after the death of the Prince Consort, and tried to make a popular success of the flower shows and band concerts.

Gradually the gardens went downhill, and in the 1880s were slowly covered with buildings. The 1851 memorial now stands at the back of the Royal Albert Hall. One of the bandstands was taken to Clapham Common.

45

45 Edward Prince of Wales (1841–1910)

This *carte de visite* photograph of the Prince with his family, was taken in 1868, soon after the birth of the Princess Victoria in July. The other children are Prince George (King George V) standing on the bench, the Princess Louise on the other side of Princess Alexandra and Prince Albert Victor, the oldest, who died of influenza in 1892.

The Prince and Princess liked Cole and understood him. The Princess would greet Cole with her marvellous smile and say: 'I hope Old King Cole is quite well.' A few weeks after this photograph was taken, the Prince of Wales visited Edinburgh and discussed Cole with Professor Playfair [28] at dinner one night. Playfair, kind as ever, told Cole about the conversation in a letter: 'He spoke gratefully of how you had carried out and developed his fathers ideas & with more thought than I believed he had given to the subject explained how opposition to you at different times had arisen & how unjust they were who did not see that you had a single eye to the public good.'

The Prince Consort was in the habit of saying to his children: 'When you want steam, you must get Cole!' The whole family grew up knowing of Cole's association, even friendship, with their father. They knew him to be the author of *The Home Treasury*, which they read in the nursery. He showed them round the Great Exhibition of 1851, and round the one in Paris of 1855. And, of course, they often visited South Kensington.

The Prince of Wales was just twenty when his father died, and had carried out very few public engagements on his own. One of these, however, had happened about eighteen months before, when Cole had arranged for him to lay the foundation stone of the Lambeth School of Art. The Prince was always ready to help Cole at South Kensington, and with his other reforms.

The Queen at first refused to allow the Prince to succeed his father as president of the Society of Arts, but in 1863 he was elected and Cole was brought nearer to him. The Prince was chairman of the committee to build the Royal Albert Hall [47], and was President of the 1851 Commissioners. He was also President of the Commission for the Paris International Exhibition of 1867. At one of the meetings of the Commission, held at Marlborough House, Cole got him to be the first royal personage to sign an international convention for the exchange of reproductions of works of art. Cole had known about electrotyping and casting in the 1840s, and reproductions had been part of the early Circulating Collections.

Cole went to spend a weekend at Sandringham in the autumn of 1873. He travelled from London in a special train with the equerries. At dinner on Sunday night 'I was placed on the Princess' right hand with much consideration. The Boys were present & played with their Mother at dinner tickling her ear &c which she bore patiently. The Prince gave me leave to go to bed at 11.30.' Cole noted the informality of the household. The Prince showed his visitors to their rooms himself, and later took Cole on a tour of the house, even into his own bed room and bathroom and those of the Princess. Cole tried to persuade her to play in a public concert at the Albert Hall, with the Orchestral Society. Cole wrote that: 'She said "not till I am Mrs Queen Cole". Her naive loveliness is engaging and her beauty is charming.'

During what can be called Cole's sewage period, he advised the Prince on modernising the drains at Sandringham. When Cole was there on a visit, the whole house-party were taken by the prince to view the drains, and the Prince lifted a little trap-door, and was delighted by the way the gas jet was drawn downwards by the draught.

On the day Cole died he received a letter from the Prince in support of his idea to found Guilds of Health in towns.

46 General, the Honble, Charles Grey (1804–1870)

After the death of the Prince Consort, the Queen, for the first time, appointed a private secretary. She chose the man who was one of her oldest friends, and who had been the Prince's secretary, General Grey.

He was the second son of the 2nd Earl Grey, who was Prime Minister at the time of the Reform Bill, and who had fifteen children. They were a powerful noble Whig family of the old sort and friends of the Queen. When he was sixteen, Charles joined the Rifle Brigade and by buying and exchanging commissions rose to be a full general in 1865. Before the Queen's accession, he sat in Parliament as a Whig, but on coming to the throne she immediately appointed him an equerry, and his sister Louise, who was married to Lord Durham, a lady of the bedchamber. Grey was one of the small party who went to Gotha in January 1840 to escort Prince Albert to England for his marriage, and from 1849, he was his private secretary.

Grey was a very important ally for Cole, especially after the death of the Prince, as Cole did not have the personal contact with the Queen that he had had with her husband. She wished to continue the Prince's work for science and art, but it was Grey who discussed projects with her and acted as a go-between for people like Cole.

He helped to get the Horticultural Society's gardens finished and sat on the committee that oversaw the placing of the prince's statue on the memorial to the Great Exhibition. He obtained the Queen's approval for the building of the Albert Hall [47], when the Commissioners were reluctant to commit themselves, and he lent his personal prestige to it by becoming one of its treasurers.

As can be seen from this portrait, Grey carried himself like a soldier. He was said to have 'a masculine mind, of great readiness and sound sense'. He was married with six children and surrounded by a crowd of relations. The husband of one of his many nieces wrote that he was always 'most trusting and open in all matters', and went on to say that 'he had been to the Queen the frankest and ablest adviser, and had worked with a never flagging energy in her service'.

46

47 The Royal Albert Hall

Cole once said: 'in my opinion, Music unites in the highest degree both Science and Art'. From the time when he was quite a small boy and his father gave him a 'black ebony flute with silver keys', he was deeply moved by music. Most of all he enjoyed really large choral works by Bach or Handel. Prince Albert was a talented musician, as a performer and a composer, and he and Cole both wished to bring music to South Kensington. In 1858, while Cole was in Italy, he drew up plans for The Chorus Hall Company, which would have built a hall, but it came to nothing. A year or so later, Cole and Dilke tried to include music in the London International Exhibition of 1862. Fowke designed a very large concert hall as part of the exhibition buildings, which, in the end had to be excluded as there was not enough money for it.

During the summer of 1861, Cole and the Prince Consort met for the last time. They stood together near the place where the hall was later built and the Prince 'expressed his hopes that some day there should be built a central hall of Arts and Sciences'.

Within a month of the Prince's death, the Queen appointed a committee, with Lord Derby as chairman, to advise her on the national memorial to the Prince, using the money subscribed by the public. The committee recommended a memorial and a hall, and in June 1862, Cole, who was not on the committee, went to Windsor to discuss the report with General Grey: 'The Queen sent down to ask when I proposed to go back to town, and then to say she would see me about two. Grey and I went up to the Prince's room. His hat and gloves were laid out in the accustomed way, and his desk table looked just as it used to do. The Queen came in—looked calm and collected. Asked me if I thought

47

the suggestion for the Memorial was practical. Said she had no taste—used only to listen to him—not worthy to untie his latchet.'

When the likely cost of the Albert Memorial was known, it became clear that there would not be enough money in the fund for both it and a hall. But Cole refused to give up, and it was the Queen's support, encouraged by Grey, that made the scheme possible. Lord Derby, who was President of the 1851 Commissioners, and who became Prime Minister in 1866, opposed Cole, whose ways he had known for twenty years. Lord Granville told Cole that: 'Lord Derby had no faith in the Hall. but as the Queen wished it inquiries might be made if authorized by Finance Comtee but cd not do it alone.'

In the Spring of 1863 the Commissioners agreed to reserve the site, opposite where the memorial was to be. In the Autumn, Cole and Fowke, who already had the idea of an eliptical building in their minds, went to the South of France and visited the Roman amphitheatres at Nimes and Arles. Back in London, Fowke made designs, with Gilbert Redgrave, as an assistant, and Sergeant

Spackman made a model. There was a pause. The Commissioners wondered whether to build a small hall of their own, suitable for meetings of learned societies, but not suitable for Cole's grand choral works. In August 1864 Cole lost patience, and began to collect money from investors. He wrote to General Grey: 'I have come to the conclusion that the only way to get the Memorial Hall done is to *do* it! . . . I don't intend to be beaten in this Matter and I intend to have the thing so advanced that please God and the Queen, the first stone may be laid perhaps with that of the personal memorial.' By January 1865, Cole had collected a list of seventy high-sounding names of subscribers for seats in the hall. A few had promised to take as many as ten seats at £100 each. The boxes cost £1,000. Cole and Redgrave went down to Osborne, and enlisted the support of the Prince of Wales, who consented to be president and to call a meeting of the subscribers at Marlborough House, to elect a provisional committee. This did not happen until July, but in the meantime, Lord Derby, who was perhaps influenced by the royal enthusiasm for the scheme, was won over. Abandoning their own hall,

48

which would have cost them £100,000, the Commissioners granted a lease of 999 years on the land, at 1/– a year, and subscribed £50,000 towards the building costs, on condition that the total did not exceed £200,000.

On the 20 May 1867, the Queen performed one of her first public engagements since the death of the Prince Consort over six years before, and laid the foundation stone for the hall.

This photograph, which belonged to Cole, shows the hall under construction, most probably in the summer of 1868, and was taken from the top of the Albert Memorial. Fowke's Great Conservatory, and the Horticultural Gardens are in the background.

The hall was built in the South Kensington style of dark red brick, with dark joints, off-set by fawn coloured terra-cotta mouldings. Fowke's design was taken over, after his death, by General Scott [37], who added the mosaic frieze. Seven artists, including J C Horsley and Poynter, made designs, co-ordinated by Scott. Working drawings were

prepared by Sergeant Spackman, who projected the designs on to a wall, and then drew round them.

Cole arranged a sumptuous opening ceremony for 29 March 1871, when the Queen came with full state ceremonial. She wrote in her journal: 'Good Mr. Cole was quite crying with emotion and delight. . . . I had never been at such a big function since beloved Albert's time, and it was naturally trying and "émotionnant" for me.'

48   The Loggia of the Cole Building

This most Italian arcaded loggia, overlooking Exhibition Road, was Cole's idea, and in supervising Scott's design of the building, he made sure it was carried out. Perhaps in deference to his being the originator of it, some of the terra-cotta columns are decorated with the Cole family arms. The fourth column from the left carries the shield and crest,

49

with above them the motto 'Regem Serva Deum Cole'. Though meant to be a place where the students could work in the open air, the loggia also gave them a good view of two of Cole's other concerns at that time: the Horticultural Gardens and the Albert Hall.

The building went up between 1868 and 1872, at about the same time as the Albert Hall. It was intended to house the School of Naval Architecture, but no sooner had the school moved in than it moved out again to Greenwich. Then it was used for the Normal School for Science, with the brilliant scientist, Professor T H Huxley, as Dean. Later it was named the Huxley Building in his memory, and remained part of Imperial College until the mid-1970's when it became part of the museum.

49 Sir Joseph Whitworth (1803–1887)

This stiff portrait of a sad old man gives a poor impression of the famous inventor and arms manufacturer. In fact, at the age of sixty six, which he is in the picture, he was full of energy and commuting between his London office and his works outside Manchester.

Towards the end of their lives, Sir Joseph, who was made a baronet in 1869, and Sir Henry, who was knighted in 1875, were close friends. Cole often stayed with Whitworth at his enormous house at Stancliffe, near Matlock in Derbyshire, and in London they dined together at the Reform Club. Cole was executor of Whitworth's will and might have had the task of distributing his enormous fortune to charities. In the event, however, Whitworth outlived Cole by five years.

Whitworth was the son of a schoolmaster and ran away from a boring job when he was sixteen to work in a machine shop. After some time working in London he set himself up in Manchester in 1833. He soon became well known for his inventions that improved lathes and other machines. It was he who persuaded the engineering industry to use screws of a uniform thread, instead of each firm using its own pattern, which had led to difficulties and inefficiency.

He joined the Society of Arts in 1844, when a group of patent lawyers was trying to revive it. Patents, or 'rights of inventors', was a subject of the greatest interest to Whitworth. While Cole was Chairman of the Society in 1850–51, a great deal of work was done to bring about reform in the patent laws. Cole helped the campaign by giving Charles Dickens a memorandum that he had written, which Dickens used when he wrote 'A poor Man's Tale of a Patent', published in *Household Words* in October 1850. Until the law was changed, it took nearly forty different steps, and visits to five different government departments to obtain a patent, and each one had to be signed by the Sovereign. The system had not been changed since the Middle Ages. Dickens poked fun at the problems, and the general public heard of them. As a result the first Patent Act became law in 1852.

Whitworth's inventions were first seen at the Great Exhibition and they immediately made him famous. When Cole went with Redgrave and Fowke to visit his works a few years later, he wrote in his diary that Whitworth had 'a superb establishment', and it was 'the centre of the world for machinery'.

Whitworth made important improvements in rifles and later in long range guns, and though the War Office was slow to use his new designs, they were adopted by the French and other foreign governments.

In 1868, at Cole's suggestion, he funded thirty scholarships in practical science, which were administered by Cole's department. He also offered a prize for an essay on 'Thrift' through the Society of Arts, at a time when Cole was interested in domestic economy.

Whitworth had many honours. He received

honorary degrees from universities both in England and abroad. He was given the French Legion of Honour in 1867. He was a Fellow of the Royal Society and President of the Institute of Civil Engineers. The Society of Arts awarded him the Albert Medal in 1868.

50 The third Duke of Sutherland (1828–1892)

The board meetings of Scott's Sewage Company were held by the Duke of Sutherland at Stafford House, overlooking Green Park, 'the finest private mansion in the metropolis', which housed the Sutherland collection of pictures in a specially built gallery, 136 feet long, and boasted a 'great dining-room worthy of Versailles'. In the midst of all this grandeur, the drains intruded, and Lord Stafford, the duke's son, more than once complained to Cole of 'stinks' in his bedroom. The house is nowadays called Lancaster House and is used for government entertaining and 'summit' meetings.

The duke was not always a willing chairman of the sewage company. In the spring of 1877, when the Bank of England refused to lend capital, the duke thought that he would not risk his money either, but Cole was firm: 'I then argued with him that as a Duke in such a national object *he* must be sole guarantor & be protected by sub-guarantors.' The duke signed away £5,000 a fortnight later. He was pleased when Cole told him that he would be 'King of Cleanliness for the country'.

The duke lived mainly at Dunrobin Castle, Sutherland, or at the huge Italianate palace built by his father near Stoke-on-Trent, Trentham Hall. Cole was taken by Herbert Minton [23] to see Trentham in 1856, and noted that the 'Gardens & Corridor [are] rather imposing: but not the rooms. much cost but little effect'. At the time of the sewage company, the duke had Cole to stay at Trentham several times, and he enjoyed himself. The family was attentive, and Lord Stafford mixed him 'Lemon & Iced Water & a little Gin: wh: was refreshing'. Another time Cole was 'Threatened with a Sore throat but stopped by four glasses of Champagne'. The agent told him of the enormous cost of the duke's sumptuous hospitality. He spent over £30,000 a year on visitors and their servants. His own staff cost him £100 a year for each man-servant, £50 a year for a maid, and £100 for a horse. At that time, there were fifty gardeners employed in the grounds at Trentham, and thirty indoor servants came to family prayers when Cole stayed there.

The family name of the Dukes of Sutherland is Leveson-Gower, and the third duke was a young cousin of Lord Granville [27], who took him with

50

him on his special mission to Moscow in 1856. Though the duke was a member of one of the most influential Whig families, he was not much interested in politics. He sat in the House of Commons as a Liberal member for Sutherland, but after inheriting the dukedom, he preferred managing his estates to sitting in the House of Lords. He was the largest landowner in the British Isles, owning over 1,000,000 acres in Sutherland alone, besides land in Ross-shire, Shropshire, Staffordshire and York-shire. His estates brought him in over £141,000 a year, which was less than the Dukes of Buccleuch, Devonshire and Northumberland, or the Marquess of Bute received from smaller acreages. Much of the Duke of Sutherland's land was exceptionally poor. The first and second dukes had begun work to improve the Highland estates, and the third Duke went on and spent many hundreds of thousands of pounds on land drainage, and on building a railway. His grandfather had constructed the first road in

TRAINING SCHOOL FOR MUSIC
25 DECR 1877
Rochdale Main
DRAINAGE
Merry Xmas
Church of England
CEMENT
SOPHISTRY

51

Sutherland. He was also 'a shrewd industrial magnate', owning steel works, coal mines and mineral quarries. He was philanthropic and lent money at very low interest rates to help worth-while projects, such as the building of the ferry at Stromeferry on Loch Carron. He had a lighter side: he enjoyed driving his own steam train, and was interested in fire-fighting to the point of serving on the jury to award prizes for fire engines at the 1862 International Exhibition. One of the odder things that he did was to allow Seymour Haden [39] to hold his private view of coffins at Stafford House.

It is ironic that Lord Stafford, about ten years after he became the fourth duke, had to abandon Trentham, driven out by the intolerable stench of the river Trent that flowed close to the house, bringing with it all the sewage from Stoke-on-Trent. The duke tried to give the house to the town, but it was declined. In the summer of 1911 the house was sold to a demolition firm, and a two-day auction sale was held of the house for building materials. The tower, five storeys high, was bought in at £50, and the fittings of the Duchess's bedroom, dressing-room and boudoir only fetched £40. 'There was a remarkable dearth of buyers.'

51 Sewage works at Rochdale

This water colour was sent to Sir Henry as a Christmas card in 1877 by Frank Fowke, and it shows how funny his young relations thought his activities at that time. Cole, waves his umbrella towards the main sewer of Rochdale, from which pour Pounds, Shillings and Pence into a bed of red-hot coals, where an unconcerned demon is mixing cement. Dr Newman, sitting on a bag of ammonic fimus, tugs Sir Henry by the toe towards Roman Catholicism. Over Cole's head, cherubim trumpet the Training School for Music.

Cole used to call on Dr Newman who lived at Edgbaston, and discuss his writings and sermons with him. Cole's family half-wondered whether he might become a convert. He always said, though, that he had become an agnostic, while a very young man, under the influence of T L Peacock.

Ammonic fimus was a high-nitrogen fertiliser, and a by-product of Scott's process for treating sewage, and Cole was able to send bags of it as presents to such people as the Prince of Wales and Lord Granville.

52 The Honble (Edward) Frederick Leveson-Gower (1819–1907)

Frederick Leveson-Gower was a younger brother of Lord Granville [27]. Cole first got to know him in 1856, when they were arranging for one of the Sapper photographers from South Kensington, Corporal Spackman, to go with Lord Granville's mission to Russia. Leveson-Gower was an attaché on that mission, and later acted as his brother's secretary. All through his life he seems to have been overshadowed by his famous brother: he sat as a Member of Parliament for Stoke-on-Trent and then for Bodmin, but he was never an active or successful politician. When Gladstone wanted to make him Postmaster General, he declined saying that it might look like a 'job'.

Leveson-Gower's wife died in 1858, and though only forty, he did not remarry. As the *Dictionary of National Biography* says: '. . . it was as a social figure that he was most conspicuous. Gifted with agreeable manners, conversational tact, and a good memory, he excelled as a diner-out and giver of dinners.' He took a house in South Audley Street, and had a French chef, Monsieur Béguinot, who had been with the Duc de Morny, and so his dinners were very good indeed. Not for long, however, because M. Béguinot soon left him to work for his grander brother.

Leveson-Gower's social position, love of serious food, and lack of official employment, made him the ideal chairman of the committee for the school of cookery. The first meeting was held in July 1873, when the Prince of Wales agreed to be patron, the Duke of Westminster (another of the Leveson-Gower ducal cousins) became President, and Leveson-Gower was elected chairman. The enterprise was a success. Leveson-Gower wrote about it in *Bygone Years*, published in 1905:

> As a rule the wealthy alone derive any benefit from good cookery, and until our School was inaugurated, no systematic attempt had been made to improve it. Sir Henry's idea was therefore excellent, and it has, in spite of some ridicule and prejudice, been most extensively carried out. Schools on our model have been started in most of the chief towns in the country, . . . as well as in America and in our Colonies. . . . Since its opening nearly 100,000 pupils have there received instruction; we have further awarded about 1,700 diplomas to teachers. . . . we are teaching sick-room cookery in the London & Guy's Hospitals, to the Queen's Jubilee Nurses, in the Royal Naval Hospital at Haslar and Plymouth. . . . We teach cookery to prison warders. . . . in 1901 we revised the workhouse diets, and published a

52

> *Manual of Workhouse Cookery*, which the Local Government Board has issued to Boards and Guardians of the Poor. When to this is added what the other schools of cookery have done, the benefit to the community must already be incalculable.

Leveson-Gower pointed out that all this was achieved without any government help and he pays tribute to the work done by Edith Nicolls, the Lady Superintendent, who was the grand-daughter of T L Peacock, and a *protegée* of Cole's. Leveson-Gower often had Cole to stay at his country house in Surrey. There he met his old friend from the 1820s Mrs Grote, and listened to her play the piano.

53

53 A group of the staff at South Kensington in about 1860

Only a few of the gentlemen in this photograph can be identified. Captain Francis Fowke is in the middle, with Cole to the left and Captain John Donnelly lounging on the right. On the other side of Cole is Norman MacLeod, the Chief of the MacLeods, who had left his castle on the Isle of Skye to become one of the administrators in the Department, and who succeeded Cole as Secretary. The very young man sitting on the ground on the left is Cole's second son, Alan.

The fact that Fowke is sitting in the middle may indicate that the group is the 1st Middlesex Volunteer Engineers, which he started in November 1859. This was the time when war in Europe made the fear of invasion very real and volunteer companies were being formed all over the country. The South Kensington detachment had the advantage of good training officers ready to hand. It was commanded by the MacLeod and Cole was a Sapper and a 'rear rank man'. When Fowke told the Prince Consort that Cole marched at the back he commented: 'Then he will keep the front men marching.'

54   The entrance to the museum in 1872

Here are artists, children with their governesses and other members of the public arriving at the museum on a hot afternoon during the summer of the year before Cole retired. Against the sky is the Cole Building which had just been completed as the Science Schools. Next can be seen the top storey of the official residences, which had museum galleries on the ground floor, with comfortable apartments above for four of the senior members of the staff of the Department. In 1872, the centre ones were lived in by the Coles and the Cunliffe-Owens. Captain Festing RE and Richard Thompson lived in the two smaller ones. The houses were converted into galleries at the end of the century, but their facades can still be seen on the West side of the quadrangle. The low building in the foreground was the only one designed by a professional architect in Cole's time, and it was put up in 1856 to link the 'Boilers' to the old houses already on the site. It served as the main entrance for over twenty years, before giving way to the South range of the quadrangle, which contains the library. On the left, beyond the oak tree, is one of the vans belonging to the Department of Circulation. The shed it is in abuts the house that Cunliffe-Owen lived in before the official residences were built [40].

55   'King Cole' from *Vanity Fair* 1871

This cartoon was drawn by James Tissot during the Summer of 1871 when he had just come to London to avoid the Commune in Paris. Before he established himself in England as a painter, he did this sort of work, which he left unsigned. Cole is accompanied, as he almost always was, by his Yorkshire terrier, Jim.

Cole's portrait was published in the Album of *Vanity Fair* at this time because the Society of Arts had just announced that it was giving him the Albert Medal: 'for his important services in promoting Arts, Manufacture and Commerce, especially in aiding the establishment and development of International Exhibitions, the Department of Science and Art, and the South Kensington Museum'.

Cole was not presented with the medal until the Spring of the next year, and even then there was no ceremony at the Society's house. The cause was the serious attack of Typhoid that the Prince of Wales suffered at Sandringham during the Winter.

On 6 March 1872 Cole wrote in his diary: 'To Marlborough House to see the Pr: of Wales the first time since his illness. He gave me the Albert Medal with a little speech'.

54

E2178-1932

Further reading

Sir Henry's autobiography, which he called *Fifty Years of Public Work*, was published in two volumes in 1884, two years after his death. Up to the time of the Great Exhibition he wrote it himself, but the book was completed by two of his children, Alan and Henrietta, and the latter part is hard going for the reader. However, the book does give some of Cole's speeches and articles in full, and is indispensable for any researcher.

The best account of Cole in relation to South Kensington is to be found in *The Survey of London, Volume XXXVIII*, which gives the history of the buildings at South Kensington, both those that exist today and the ones that have disappeared, such as the buildings for the 1862 International Exhibition and the Royal Horticultural Society's Gardens. The book was published in 1975 and the parts that relate to Cole were written by Peter Bezodis and Nicholas Taylor. More about Cole will be found in John Physick's *The Victoria and Albert Museum—The History of its Building*. For Cole's work in re-organising the art schools one must turn to Janet Minihan's *The Nationalization of Culture*, published in 1977. Chapter four 'Cole and Company', gives a most readable and scholarly account of his work. Sir Henry Trueman Wood, in his *History of the Royal Society of Arts*, (1913), writes of Cole from personal knowledge, and gives an account of his connection with the Society. The *Journal* of the Society, that Cole helped to found, has many references to him and his projects. A more modern history of the Society was written by Derek Hudson and the Society's Secretary, Kenneth Luckhurst, and published to commemorate the bi-centenary in 1954. Articles about Sir Henry include: K J Fielding, 'Charles Dickens and the Department of Practical Art', *The Modern Language Review*, Volume 48 (1953). A G C Bennett, 'Ten Days in Normandy in 1860', *Country Life*, 26 March, 1964. Shirley Bury, 'Felix Summerly's Art-Manufactures', *Apollo*, 15 January 1967. Elizabeth Bonython, 'A Victorian Commuter: Sir Henry Cole's life at Shere' *Country Life*, 22 April, 1982.

Index

The figures in heavy type refer to the illustrations

Albert, Prince Consort **26,** 1, 5, 6,
7, 10, 30, 31, 33, 36, 37, 41,
46, 52, 54, 55, 56, 58, 63
Albert, Prince (Duke of Clarence)
54
Alexandra, Princess of Wales
54–55
Albert Hall
see Royal Albert Hall
Albert Memorial 10, 27, 56–57, 58
Banting, William 41
Baring, Sir Francis 23
Barry, Charles 37
Bartley, George 21
Bell, John **18,** 4, 33, 52
Bentham, Jeremy 17, 19, 21
Bessborough, Earl of 35
Bond, Elizabeth (H C's aunt) 19
Bond, John James (H C's cousin)
25
British Museum 51
Brunel, Isambard Kingdom 25,
28, 31
Buller, Charles **7,** 2, 3, 17, 19, 21,
28, 35
Bulwer, Sir E. 35
Callcott, Sir Augustus 25
Callcott, Maria 15
Cambridge, Duke of 35
Carlyle, Jane 16
Carlyle, Thomas 16, 17, 18
Casey, W L 40
Chadwick, Edwin 2, 16, 31
Chadwick, Rachel 31
Christmas Card, 1st. **16,** 2
Christ's Hospital **1,** 49
Christy, I F 33
Clanricarde, Earl of 35
Clark, Sir James 9
Coalbrookdale Iron Company 33
Cobden, Richard 10, 28, 37
Cole, Alan (H C's son) 11, 21, 24,
40, 49, 63
Cole, Charles (H C's brother) 31,
35, 49
Cole, Granville (H C's son) 21
Cole, Henrietta (H C's daughter)
4, 21, 29

Cole, Henry
Birth, appearance and
character 2–3
Education 3, 14, 15, 20
Reform of the public records
3–4, 15, 18, 19
Journalism 3–5, 16, 17, 18,
19, 29, 30
Postage reform 4, 5, 19, 21–24
Improvement of Society of
Arts 5, 59
'Felix Summerly' 2, 4, 5, 24,
32, 33
Reform of Schools of Design
4, 9–10, 12
Family 4, 9, 19–20
Exhibition of 1851 1, 5–6,
30–31, 34, 36
Museum at Marlborough
House 7, 40
Duke of Wellington's funeral
car 41–43
South Kensington Museum
9, 10, 26, 44–64 *passim*
Royal Horticultural Society's
Gardens 30, 53–54
Royal Albert Hall 56–58
Public Health 10–11, 55, 60
Death 12
Cole, Captain Henry Hardy, R E
(H C's oldest son) 11, 21, 49
Cole, Henry Robert (H C's father)
2
Cole, Isabella (H C's daughter)
21, 46
Cole, Laetitia (H C's daughter)
4, 21, 29
Cole (Frederick) Lindsay
(H C's brother) 31
Cole, Marian Fairman (H C's wife)
9, 2, 4, 9, 18, 19–20, 30, 34
Cole, Mary (H C's daughter) 21,
29
Cole, Richard (H C's brother) 31
Cole, Rose (H C's daughter) 11, 21
Commissioners' Estate, South
Kensington 6, 8, 10, 35, 46,
54, 57, 58

Cookery 5
Training School 11–12, 62
Cox, David 15
Cubitt, Sir William 37
Cundall Joseph 26, 28, 33
Cunliffe-Owen
see Owen
Darby, Miss 16
de la Rue, Warren 40
Derby, 14th Earl of 1, 37, 56, 57
Devonshire, Duke of 35, 37, 60
Dickens, Charles 9, 10, 22, 40, 59
Dilke, C W 6, 29, 31
Dilke, C Wentworth (1st Bart)
21, 4, 6, 30, 31, 37, 40, 46, 56
Dilke, Charles W (2nd Bart) 29
Dilke, Family 29, 49
Dilke, Maria 31
Donnelly, Major-General J F D
7, 8, 45, 46, 63
Durham, Countess of 56
Durham, Earl of 18, 56
Durham, Joseph 52
Edinburgh, Duke of 11
Edward, Prince of Wales (King
Edward VII) **45,** 2, 9, 10, 11,
20, 45, 52, 57, 61, 62, 64
Ellison, Richard 26
Exhibition, Fisheries, London
1883 45
Exhibition, International,
London 1851 **30,** 1, 2, 5, 6, 7,
19, 27, 29, 30, 32, 34, 35, 36,
40, 45, 54, 55, 59
Memorial to: **42,** 54, 56
Exhibition, International,
London 1862 5, 10, 30, 31, 35,
36, 46, 50, 54, 56, 61
Illustrations of **40, 44**
Exhibition, International,
Paris 1855 9, 32, 45, 46, 55
Exhibition, International,
Paris 1867 49
Exhibition, Paris 1849 5–6
Exhibitions, Society of Arts 5,
24, 30, 33
Festing, Major-General E R 7, 8,
64

Fowke, Captain Francis, R E **36**, 8, 10, 47, 52, 54, 56, 57, 58, 59, 63
Fowke, Frank 21, 46, 61
Fowke, Mrs Francis 46
Fox, Charles 37
George, Prince (King George V) 54
Gilbert, W S *Pirates of Penzance* 7–8
Gladstone, W E 45–62
Gower, Lady Florence 12
Graham, John 16
Grant, Horace 16, 31
Granville, 2nd Earl **27**, 6, 7, 20, 30, 31, 34, 35, 36, 37, 45, 51, 57, 60, 61, 62
Granville, Countess 35
Great Exhibition
    See Exhibition, International, London 1851
Greville, Charles 35
Grey, General Charles **46**, 10, 34, 52, 54, 56, 57
Grote George 16, 17, 18
Grote, Harriet 17, 62
Haden, Deborah (née Whistler) 49
Haden, Francis Seymour **39**, 9, 25, 29, 61
Hickson, William 17
Hill, Edwin 40
Hill, Rowland **11**, 4, 30
Holland and Co 33
Horsley, John Callcott 2, 25, 33, 58
Horsley William 25
Houghton, Lord 2
Hughes, Family 16
Huxley, Prof. T H 59
Imperial College 12, 59
Jennens and Bettridge 33
Jewsbury, Geraldine 16
Jim (H C's dog) 32, 64
Jones, Owen 40
Knocker, Lieut.,—R E 54
Labouchere, Henry 26
Langdale, Lord **8**, 3, 21
Lawrence, Sir Thomas 25
Leader, John Temple 17
Leopold, King of the Belgians 26
Leveson-Gower, The Honble (Edward) Frederick **52**, 11
Liebig, Baron von 36
Linnell, John 24, 28
Lloyd, Col. J A, R E 37
Louise, Princess 54
Lowe, Robert **41**, 10
MacLeod, The 63
Maclise, Daniel 4, 28
Maitland Family 19–20
Marlborough House, 7, 8, 9
    Museum at **32**, 7, 41

Maw-Egley, William 44
Mill, Harriet 17
Mill, James 17, 19
Mill, John Stuart **5**, 2, 3, 4, 16, 17, 18, 28
Minto, Earl of 35
Minton, Herbert **23**, 5, 6, 32, 36, 44, 60
Minton & Co 27, 32, 33, 47
Molesworth, Sir William, Bart **6**, 2, 3, 21, 28
Morpeth, Viscount 35
Mulready, William **14**, 4, 23
Music 5, 15, 16, 56, 57
    National Training School for 8, 11, 61
    Royal College of 11, 12
Newman, Dr Henry 61
Nicolls, Edith 62
Owen, Francis Philip Cunliffe **35**, 7, 45, 47, 50–51, 64
Owen, Col. Henry Cunliffe, R E 7, 37, 45, 46
Palgrave, Elizabeth (née Turner) 15
Palgrave, Sir Francis **2**, 3
Palmerston, Lord 34
Paxton, Joseph 6, 37, 40
Peacock, Thomas Love **4**, 3, 17, 61, 62
Peel, Sir Robert 36, 37
Pellatt & Co 33
Photography 8–9
Playfair, Lyon **28**, 6, 7, 9, 31, 40, 45, 55
Postage Reform 4, 11, 12, 13, 21–24
Poynter, Edward 26, 58
Public Health 5, 55, 60
    Sewage 15, 11, 55
    see also Scott's Sewage Company
Public Records 3–4, 15, 18, 19, 34
Radnor, Earl of 35
Railways 4, 28
Redgrave, Gilbert 57
Redgrave, Richard **17**, 4, 7, 10, 33, 36, 41, 44, 45, 46, 47, 51, 59
Reid, William 6, 27, 40
Robinson, (John) Charles **34**, 2, 7, 40
Robinson, Marian 9
Roebuck, John 2, 16
Ross, Sir William 33
Royal Albert Hall **47**, 1, 10, 12, 32, 46, 47, 51, 54, 55, 56, 59
Royal College of Art 12
    see also Schools of Design
Royal College of Music 11, 12
Royal Commission for 1851 6, 30, 36, 37, 47, 54, 55, 56, 57

Royal Engineers (Sappers) 7–8, 21, 51
    Volunteers 63
Royal Horticultural Society 30, 47, 54
    Gardens **43, 44**, 30, 46, 47, 52, 56, 58, 59
Royal Society of Arts
    see Society of Arts
Rue, Warren de la
    see De la Rue
Ruskin, John 10, 12
Russell, Alice 31
Russell, Lord John 37
Russell, John Scott **22**, 5, 6, 30–33, 37
Salisbury, 2nd Marquess of 9
Schools of Design (of Art) 4, 6, 8, 9, 11, 26, 32, 34, 35, 41, 44, 51, 55
Science Museum 8, 9, 12
Scott, Major-General H Y D **37**, 7, 8, 9, 10, 46, 58
Scott, Selina 47
Scott's Sewage Company 10–11, 47, 60
Sewage
    see under Public Health *and* Scott's Sewage Company
Sheepshanks, John 24, 26, 46, 52
Shere, Surrey (H C's cottage at) **38**, 47, 49
Smirke, Sydney 52
Smith, Benjamin 33
Society of Antiquaries 3, 45
Society of Arts 2, 5, 11, 22, 24, 27, 29–30, 31, 32–33, 34, 40, 55, 59, 60, 64
Soulages Collection 32
South Kensington Estate
    see Commissioners' Estate South Kensington
South Kensington Museum **40, 42, 48, 52**, 1, 8, 9, 10, 12, 26, 32, 35, 40, 46, 47, 50, 51, 52, 64
Spackman, Sergeant Benjamin, R E 35, 57, 58
Stafford, Marquess of (4th Duke of Sutherland) 60, 61
Stephen, Laura 29
Stephen, Leslie 29
Stephenson, Robert 37
Sterling, John 16
Stockmar, Baron 34
Sullivan, Arthur 8, 11
Summerly, Felix (H C's pseudonym)
    Art Manufactures **24, 25**, 4, 5, 24, 26, 27, 28, 31
    Christmas Card **16**, 2
    Guide Books 4
    Home Treasury **19**, 4, 11, 24, 25, 26, 28, 29, 55